MUSCLE BUILDING 101

The Fundamentals of Shaping Your Physique

By Robert Kennedy and Dwayne Hines II

ROBERT KENNEDY'S
MUSCLEMAG International

Published by MuscleMag International
6465 Airport Road
Mississauga, Ontario
Canada L4V 1E4

Designed by Jackie Kydyk
Edited by Mandy Morgan

Canadian Cataloguing in Publication Data

Kennedy, Robert, 1938-
   Muscle building 101 : the fundamentals of shaping
your physique

Includes bibliographical references and index.
ISBN 1-55210-008-1

   1. Bodybuilding. I. Hines, Dwayne, 1961-
II. Title.

GV546.5.K457 1997   646.7'5   C97-901205-8

Distributed in Canada by
Canbook Warehouse
1220 Nicholson Road
Newmarket, Ontario
Canada L3Y 7V1
800-399-6858

Distributed in the States by
BookWorld Services
1933 Whitfield Park Loop
Sarasota, Florida 34243
800-444-2524

Printed in Canada

The Fundamentals of Shaping Your Physique

By Robert Kennedy and Dwayne Hines II

TABLE OF CONTENTS

INTRODUCTION TO THE ART AND SCIENCE OF SHAPING YOUR BODY

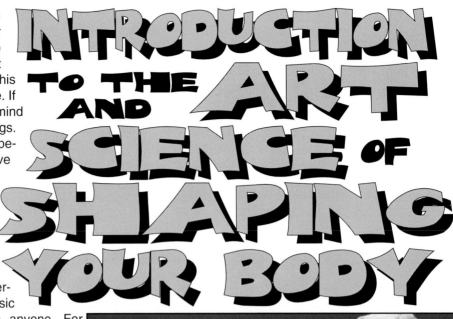

This book is an introduction to the art and science of shaping your physique. You don't have to have a head full of knowledge about building your body to profit from this book. Actually, the opposite is true. If you read this book with an open mind you will discover many new things. *Muscle Building 101* will also hopefully dispel any myths you have concerning bodybuilding (such as muscles turning into fat, or that lifting weights makes you slow). If you have been involved with bodybuilding for some time you can still profit from the material in this book because a lot of bodybuilders overlook or forget several of the basic principles. This can happen to anyone. For instance, a physique champion from a couple of years back got caught up in one type of training to the neglect of a basic principle, and lost some of the development in his back. He had to go back to the basics to change his training to get the results he wanted.[1] If that can happen to a champion bodybuilder who has won several top trophies, it can also happen to you. So even if you have been around the bodybuilding block a couple of laps you can still profit from this book. However, the main focus is on the basics of building your body. If you want to read advanced information there are hundreds of books on the market. But if you want to get into the fundamentals of how you can change the shape of your body, this is the book for you.

Aaron Baker

Everyone can benefit from bodybuilding – everyone! You can use bodybuilding to benefit your physique in thousands of different ways. Famed martial artist **Bruce Lee** had his weight-training equipment shipped to him on location – he took his training, his weight training, that serious. He knew the tremendous benefits building his body provided. No matter what sport you are in, or what goal you have for your physique, bodybuilding provides the best training vehicle to reach that goal.

Who has the best bodies in Hollywood? In the movies, you have to look great – and who looks the greatest? Three of the very best are **Arnold Schwarzenegger, Sylvester Stallone,** and **Jean-Claude Van Damme.** What do these three men have in common? They are all bodybuilders. And amazingly, **Stallone** and **Schwarzenegger** are over fifty! Bodybuilding can do wonders for your physique. If you want to look really hot,

Arnold
Schwarzenegger

you do not need a facelift – you need to take up bodybuilding. Bodybuilding is the ultimate physique-shaping and conditioning tool on planet earth.

BUILDING YOUR BODY

Bodybuilding is a very basic pursuit – it involves building the body. While that may sound simple, it is exactly what the sport and art form of bodybuilding is all about. Bodybuilding is not about "creating" a body (that was God's job) but rather about taking the body that you have and "building" it to a point far beyond what it was when you started. There are many forces that work against the body – the ravages of aging, stress, sickness, pollution, etc. While man has not found the fountain of youth, bodybuilding is the next best thing. Bodybuilding keeps the body stronger for a much longer period of time than if the body were left to drift into old age on its own, without physical training. **Arnold Schwarzenegger,** one of the most well-known personalities on the planet, said of bodybuilding and exercise, "If you exercise faithfully, with a strict adherence to form, you should notice an increase in strength and coordination within a very short time. Your joint mobility and flexibility will be better. You'll expend less energy in performing both physical and mental tasks. You'll have better posture. Your ability to relax and voluntarily reduce stress and tension will be heightened. Your heart should become stronger and your circulation improve. You'll have greater immunity from illness. You'll be better protected from injuries, and be able to heal more rapidly when one does occur." [2]

Bodybuilding is perhaps the most drastic of all sports and/or arts. While most sports and sporting activities teach a person how to better perform some physical function (such as volleyball, tennis, or softball, for instance) bodybuilding actually changes the physique in an astonishing manner. As an art form, bodybuilding is stunning – instead of working on an inert object, the body itself becomes the object. It is impressive to shape a piece of art but it is twice as impressive when that piece of art is your physique.

In bodybuilding you play a major role in determining your goals and vision for what you want to achieve with your body. In many other sports you have to follow a prescribed set of rules or do what a coach tells you. In bodybuilding there are certain fixed principles, but once you learn these, you can do what you want with them. Bodybuilding is perhaps the most creative of all sports activities. **Rick Valente,** star of the popular *Body Shaping* show on cable TV, notes about bodybuilding, "I don't believe

Lou Ferrigno and
Robby Robinson

that anything is carved in stone so I am not one of those people who says it's this way or no way. Everybody's body chemistry is a little different. What may work for you may not work for someone else. People who say it's only this way or that way really bother me."[3] Once you understand the basics of bodybuilding, you have a tremendous latitude to experiment and try new things.

BUILDING THE BODY IS PROGRESSIVE

Bodybuilding is a progressive form of training. You don't have to start off at an extremely rapid rate, and you don't necessarily have to be a superstar either. In fact, it is often the people who started training with an average or even below-par body who make the most progress. Consistency is the great equalizer in many sports, and this is especially true for bodybuilding. A consistent training approach is how you make noticeable progress. The best manner in which to train the physique is to pace yourself. You don't have to, and can't, build a superhot body in 14 days. It does take time. Your body will become bigger, stronger, and more shapely over a consistent time period of training. It is consistency that forms a champion. **Lou Ferrigno,** the "Hulk," pointed out that even he had to be consistent and patient to achieve success. "People don't believe me when I tell them my chest isn't naturally large and that I've had to work hard to bring it up. My chest was actually small and underdeveloped during my first few years of training because my arms were so long."[4] Even the best bodybuilders have obstacles to overcome and it takes patience and persistence to change the physique.

There are a lot of people who set New Year's resolutions or get a great body-training plan together only to drift away from training after a furious start. It is far better to keep your training at a consistent pace and keep it up rather than try and achieve anything substantial in short, frantic spurts.

> IT IS FAR BETTER TO KEEP YOUR TRAINING AT A CONSISTENT PACE AND KEEP IT UP RATHER THAN TRY AND ACHIEVE ANYTHING SUBSTANTIAL IN SHORT, FRANTIC SPURTS.

> ONCE YOU UNDERSTAND THE BASICS OF BODYBUILDING, YOU HAVE A TREMENDOUS LATITUDE TO EXPERIMENT AND TRY NEW THINGS.

BODYBUILDING IS COMPREHENSIVE

Bodybuilding is a comprehensive sport/activity. It is the most extensive art of training the body that has yet been devised. While many sports contain just one approach to fitness or training (running is basically running; swimming is swimming, etc.), bodybuilding includes several different aspects of fitness. Bodybuilding incorporates many activities under one banner. Some people mistakenly think that bodybuilding is just lifting weights. That is not true at all, although lifting weights is one of the central pillars of the sport. But there are others. In addition to lifting iron, bodybuilding also includes diet and nutrition, stretching, aerobic/cardiovascular work (which is itself a broad spectrum), and several other aspects. These various aspects come together to create a dynamic effect on the body that makes the body look fantastic. Each aspect will be discussed in this book as each contributes to making your body look better – which is the goal of bodybuilding. **Dorian Yates,** multi-Mr. Olympia winner stated, "When I began training a little less than 10 years ago, I immediately knew bodybuilding was for me. I read as much as I could about training, nutrition, and anything else that would help me succeed as a bodybuilder."[5] It is the successful combination of various and particular elements that produce the sum total of bodybuilding.

Dorian Yates

6

A BETTER BODY

As mentioned earlier, bodybuilding is focused on building up the body. The main goal is to build a better body. That leaves quite a bit of room for personal interpretation. For you, a better body may mean losing a couple of inches of fat off of your waist, and adding an inch or two to your arms. For another person it may mean developing the legs; for yet another it could mean competitive bodybuilding. The key is to improve your body to suit your goals and the vision you have for your physique. This is best accomplished through bodybuilding. Although many people envision competitive bodybuilding when they hear the term "bodybuilder," there are actually very few competitive bodybuilders. In fact, when compared to noncompetitive bodybuilders, the percentage of competitive bodybuilders is minuscule. What is a competitive bodybuilder? He/she is a bodybuilder who enters a contest to compete with other bodybuilders for the opportunity to win a trophy and title for having the best body. But most people who take up the sport of bodybuilding do not compete. That is, they do not compete with other people. They compete with themselves. One of the crucial factors in physique training is to continually challenge yourself. For instance, if you lifted 100 pounds last week, you would try to lift 105 pounds this week. The same holds true for body size – you want to continually work to surpass your previous best effort.

MORE MUSCLE, LESS FAT

One of the basic goals of bodybuilding is to build more muscularity and decrease body-fat. How much muscularity you build and how much fat you lose is up to you. The more muscle you add and the less fat you carry on your body, the better you will look. But your appearance centers around your definition of what looks good. You decide what type of body you want to build, then use bodybuilding as the vehicle that will take you to that body, making your goal a reality.

MUSCLE MASS

One of the goals that many people use bodybuilding for is to put on more muscle mass. Your body is primarily muscle, fat, and bone. You cannot really increase your bone size beyond a small amount, and you definitely don't want to increase the percentage of your bodyfat. That leaves one area to work on – muscle mass. Again, how much mass you add is up to you and your specific genetic potential (some people have an easier time adding muscle mass than others). Some people really like to carry a lot of muscle mass; others train for a lean and mean muscularity that is trimmer in design.

In competitive bodybuilding there are two basic approaches to building the physique – mass and aesthetics. The mass approach is just that – as much muscle mass as the body can hold. The aesthetic approach is more of a focus on the overall symmetry and flow of lean muscularity. The mass approach is the brute size and strength style; the aesthetic look is more graceful and shapely. The same styles are often seen in noncompetitive bodybuilders. They focus on one of these two approaches. Or you can do both – start with one and work into another. That is exactly what

Multi-Mr. Olympia Dorian Yates

Arnold Schwarzenegger did. He stated in his autobiography that he took his body from animal mass to a chiseled and polished look. You can do the same, or focus on either style.

BODYBUILDING AS A TOOL

You can use bodybuilding as a tool to work on whatever part of your body that is subpar. For instance, if your arms are small and weak, you can build size and strength into them with a bodybuilding program. If your legs are tiny, you can add muscle size. If you want to take fat off of your waist and build up a muscular midsection, it can be done. Any major muscle group (as well as the minor muscles) of the body can be developed through bodybuilding. You can target what you want and work on it. But the best use of bodybuilding, and the prime aim of the sport of bodybuilding, is the total development of the body. Bodybuilding is not like tennis, which leaves one arm undeveloped, or like running, which does not develop the upper body. Bodybuilding is a sport that aims at building the full body. Body symmetry is a goal. You want your right arm to look as good as your left, your upper body to be in proportion with your lower body. Bodybuilding is all about body balance – balanced muscularity. And a body with balanced muscularity looks fantastic – like a Greek statue.

> ANY MAJOR MUSCLE GROUP ON THE BODY CAN BE DEVELOPED THROUGH BODYBUILDING.

ART AND SCIENCE

Bodybuilding is an art and a science. It is a science because it operates within the boundaries of established rules and principles. It is an art because there is a lot of room for personal and unique application of those rules and principles. And bodybuilding is still very much an emerging sport and art form. A lot of new techniques and principles are still being discovered.

Gunther Schlierkamp

PRAGMATIC SPORT

Bodybuilding is very much a pragmatic sport – you work with what is discovered to be effective. Much of the original body of principles has come about from empirical studies in the gym. Empirial studies are based on practical experience, rather than theory. Observation and experimentation play a very big part in bodybuilding. There is some room for empirical work on the part of each person who picks up an iron because although the human body is very similar in many ways, there are differences that make for individual uniqueness. This means that there can sometimes be different reactions to the same stimuli. Body type, body frame, hereditary factors, ethnic factors, emotional levels, and a host of other characteristics can subtly change the reaction of the body to a training and dieting routine. In essence, every person who starts bodybuilding is an experimenter – they have to observe how the training they are engaging in works or doesn't work for their unique physique. The incredible **Dorian Yates** states, "Once I found the things that interested me, I'd give them a try in the gym. Through trial and error, I found the training system and diet that worked best for me."[6] This is what each of you must do – discover the basic theories (which are included in this book), try them out, and stick with the ones that work for you. Remember, each physique is different.

However, in spite of these subtle individual differences, there is a large body of study that has provided some general principles for training the physique. A systematic approach to building the body does exist.

SYSTEMATIC TRAINING

A systematic body of principles has been developed during the past five decades on the sport and art form of bodybuilding. These principles are used by bodybuilders to bring about definite and positive changes in the

> ONCE YOU HAVE THE BASICS OF BODYBUILDING DOWN, YOU WILL HAVE A SOLID FOUNDATIONAL BODY OF KNOWLEDGE THAT YOU CAN ALWAYS USE TO STAY IN TERRIFIC SHAPE.

Kevin Levrone and Dorian Yates

physique. These "laws of bodybuilding" have already been discovered and fine-tuned by a host of bodybuilders over the past several decades. New ideas are always emerging, but there are some principles that have stood out as being basic, proven, and true elements for shaping the physique. These principles will be presented in the next chapter. It is always good to start the study of any new area by looking at the basics surrounding that field. It is foolish to try and work with the more involved areas before you have mastered the basics. This idea is as true for bodybuilding as it is anywhere else. Once you have the basics of bodybuilding down you will have a solid founda-

Once you master the basic muscle principles you're on your way to an awesome physique.

tional body of knowledge that you can always use to stay in terrific shape. Learn the basics really well and your long-term training efforts will profit. Once you know the basics you can move on to the fancy stuff. The good part is that your body will start improving quite soon. Although big changes take quite some time to bring about, you will begin to see some physical changes within the first six weeks of training.

Approach this book with an open mind. Some of the things you have heard about bodybuilding are myths – others are fact. Discover for yourself through *Muscle Building 101* what the real deal is.

PERSONAL TRAINER

Some people rely on a personal trainer to help them get into the sport of bodybuilding. Although using a personal trainer can help (provided that he or she has the appropriate knowledge), a personal trainer can be very expensive and not always available. This book can be used as your personal trainer. The information provided in *Muscle Building 101* will give you all you need to know on how to build a superhot physique. In fact, this book will probably be better than a personal trainer because you will be provided with a systematic approach to building your body, along with the

Lenda Murray

> REMEMBER, EACH PHYSIQUE IS UNIQUE.

Nasser El Sonbaty and Sonny Schmidt

principles that lie behind the methods employed. There will also be lots of inside tips revealed, which can only enhance your training. So use *Muscle Building 101* to your advantage and build a fantastic physique!

HYPE

There is a lot of hype and false advertising in the fitness media. People take certain facts and bend them until they are no longer true. You have to sort through an enormous amount of information to find out what is real and what is a bunch of baloney. For instance, some fitness advertisements have mentioned such claims as "gain 14 pounds in 10 days," or other wild statements about certain food products that produce miraculous results. Fortunately, you can avoid these "money traps" if you simply adhere to the principles and information learned in *Muscle Building 101*. For example, you don't need to buy a special belt to sweat your fat off – you need to eat better, exercise your midsection, and perform some aerobic work. For every false claim there is a solid principle that actually works if you know what it is. *Muscle Building 101* will provide

BODYBUILDING IS THE ULTIMATE PHYSIQUE-SHAPING AND CONDITIONING TOOL ON PLANET EARTH.

Laura Binetti

you with knowledge so that the money and time you put into your training will pay off in real dividends for your physique.

GYM JAM

If you intend to get into bodybuilding you will have to have a place to work out. This may mean joining a local gym or putting together a training area of your own. Some people use their garage or a spare bedroom. Others join together in a kind of co-operation, pooling their resources to buy different pieces of equipment and necessary training items. The combined efforts of a small group of people can usually produce a fairly nice training facility.

If you join a gym make certain it has adequate equipment. This means a lot of free weights (standard barbells and dumbells) and some machines. You don't need chrome equipment – regular iron weighs the same and you will probably pay less for your gym membership. Make certain that the gym is open and is not too crowded during the hours you want to work out. (Drive by and visit the gym during the time frame you plan to exercise.)

If you are going to set up a home gym you will need a few basic pieces of equipment. A 315-pound Olympic barbell set is great, as is some interchangeable dumbells. A solid adjustable bench is also a necessity. If you can get a bench that includes a couple of attachments (for leg- back- and arm-training) that is even better. You can find a variety of companies who sell this equipment in the back of any bodybuilding magazine such as *MuscleMag International,* etc. A local sports outlet should also carry weight equipment. Make sure that the bench and the attachments you purchase are all made of sturdy metal (2+ inches), able to handle a total of at least 500 pounds.

Spending some of your hard-earned money is a good idea because it solidifies your commitment to building your body. Once you make the commitment you are ready to get started. So start by becoming very familiar with the fundamental principles of bodybuilding, which are outlined in chapter two.

References
1. Porter Cottrell, "Get Thick," *Flex* (November 1995), 115, 117.
2. Arnold Schwarzenegger and Douglas Kent Hall, *Arnold: The Education of a Bodybuilder,* (New York: Wallaby Pocket Books, 1977), 151.
3. Greg Zulak, "Star Profile: Rick Valente," *MuscleMag International* (June 1994), 215.
4. "Overheard," *MuscleMag International* (June 1993), 251.
5. "Overheard," 251.
6. "Overheard," 251.

THE FUNDAMENTAL PRINCIPLES AND TRAINING TERMINOLOGY

Bodybuilding is built upon some fundamental principles that govern the interaction between training stimulus and the body. Knowledge and application of these principles produces rewarding and progressive results; lack of knowledge and application of these principles brings about nothing more than a waste of your time. If you want to gain some muscularity and shape your body, you are wise to learn and use the basic fundamental principles.

Every sport or art form is built around key principles. A good coach and/or trainer focuses on teaching them. A good coach places strong emphasis on the fundamentals. He spends more time with his students going over the basics and does not move ahead until the basics are grasped. This approach is also true for bodybuilding success. Many of the champions return again and again to the basics. The basics are the keys to bodybuilding success! Learning the basics is very important. Once you know the basics you will have a firm foundation for all of your

Dorian Yates and Lee Haney

Lee Priest

future physique training. **Dorian Yates,** currently the top bodybuilder in the world, stated at a recent seminar, "Stick to the basic exercises."[1] Almost all top bodybuilders will give the same advice. **Lee Priest,** a top-level bodybuilder, favors the basics.[2] **Achim Albrecht,** a winner of a world champion bodybuilding amateur title, states, "Nowadays bodybuilders have many complicated ideas about training and diet. But this is not the approach that works best for me. For my body and my personality, what I need is to stick to the fundamentals – basic exercises and free weights."[3] Remember, it is the basics that build the body.

Training the physique to bring it to an advanced level is a process, not an instantaneous event. Reaching a goal generally takes time, no matter what the sport. You are not instantly given a black belt in karate (at least not by a good instructor). The same time frame for excellence holds true in wrestling. In fact, one top coach, **Bobby Douglas,** noted that championship wrestling "can't be done overnight; there are no shortcuts; and there is no instant success."[4] This can be applied to top-level bodybuilding – you cannot add 60 pounds of muscle in a month. It will take some time and effort to achieve your goals. It takes knowledge of the basic fundamental principles to make the quickest progress possible. One young man was given a weight set by his father and worked out with the weights daily. But all he received for his effort was a lot of pain. He learned later that the body needs at least 48 hours of time off between workouts for each muscle group worked. Once he knew this and started to take time off between workouts he began to progress rapidly. It wasn't his amount of effort that had held him back; it was his lack of knowledge of some of the basic and key principles in bodybuilding which had prevented him from quicker progress. You can avoid his mistake if you take the time to learn the basic fundamental principles that are listed in this chapter. And be an active participant in the process. Think through why a principle works in one instance and not in another. Pay attention to your body's response to the training and dietary principles. Get a notebook and write down what you discover about your physique and how it responds to training stimuli.

Achim Albrecht and Milos Sarcev

1. *Learn the basics* before you move on to the fancy stuff. The basics are the keys for building the body. The fancy stuff is just fine tuning, which can be added later.

2. *Actively involve your mind in the process*. The mind is the most important muscle, so to speak. Contrary to the myth, bodybuilding is not a sport for dummies. Think through the whys and hows of training as you train.

3. *Train hard*. Apply some action to the training basics in the gym. One of the best traits you can bring to the gym is a good "hard work ethic." Bodybuilding is not a sport for a sissy. You can expect some pain in the gym. Muscularity is developed, not given.

4. *Believe you can achieve your goals*. A positive attitude goes a long way in the gym. You are going to provide the motivation for your training so believe you can achieve what you set out to do. Whether you believe you can or you can't, you are right.

> **THE BASICS ARE THE KEYS TO BODYBUILDING SUCCESS!**

Pay close attention to the fundamental training principles listed in the following pages of this chapter. Read through them more than once. Read the chapter again as you progress into your workout. Some of the concepts will become clear as you lift the weights, diet, and trim the fat off of your physique. Mentally digest each concept as you use it in your bodybuilding training endeavors.

RADICAL CHANGE

It was mentioned previously that the change bodybuilding brings to the body is gradual. However, that does not mean the change is minor. The changes bodybuilding can produce in the physique are drastic and radical. You can literally add several inches of muscle to your body and lose several inches over a period of time. The advertising that promotes "getting massive muscles in a month" is partially right and partially wrong. You won't get massive in a month, but if you trained for a sustained period of time you will build much bigger muscles and lose a lot of fat. The transformation to your physique will be radical. As noted earlier, bodybuilding is the quickest way to make some extremely positive changes to your body. How far you take it is up to you. There are some very amazing things you can accomplish with your body through bodybuilding. Some professional bodybuilders have chests that are close to 60 inches around and arms that are over 22 inches in diameter. You may or may not be impressed by that, but the upside potential for muscular change is tremendous. You don't have to get drastic, but the possibility for awesome change (to the body) is there within you. Bodybuilding brings it out. You can basically gear your physique gains toward whatever you want. Some choose to add some muscle and lose some fat. Others want to make their muscles as big as they can; yet others have aspirations for competing in contests. Some people take up bodybuilding to build a stronger and more fit physique. What you do with the tremendous tool of bodybuilding is up to you. The following principles will tell you how.

Roland Kickinger

PROGRESSIVE ADAPTATION AND OVERLOAD

The first principle to know about building your body is that of progressive adaptation. The body is a complex and wonderful creation. It is equipped to handle outside stress, provided the stress is not too overwhelming. When the body is faced with a physical challenge that takes it beyond where it has been before, it responds by making the muscles bigger and stronger to handle the next perceived challenge. An overload causes the body to regroup and put together a response that will give it the necessary firepower to handle any similar future demand. The primary element that the body responds with are the muscles, although there does seem to be a small response in other areas like the bones. The body will provide this response when there is an increased demand. This demand is called the overload. For the body to react in a positive manner this overload must be slight. An overload that is too large will not stimulate the body's positive response but rather cause injury to the body. For instance, if you were normally able to pick up 100 pounds and then lift 110 pounds, your body would come back in a couple of days stronger (provided you gave it adequate rest and nutrition) for the next challenge. But if you tried to pick up 700 pounds, you would most likely injury your body or be unable to meet the challenge. For the overload principle/technique to work, you have to only use a slight overload. Too much of an overload and you will waste your effort. It is essential to keep the overload just slightly more difficult than the previous challenge.

The late Andreas Munzer

Your body will respond to a slight overload with more muscularity. As you continue to use the overload principle/technique, your body will continue to adapt to the new challenges with more and more muscularity. This is the principle of progressive adaptation. As the body faces a gradual series of slightly more difficult challenges, it gradually builds the muscles up. It progressively adapts (with new muscularity) to the overload it is presented with.

It is essential for you to use the overload/progressive adaptation principle to make changes in your physique. If you continue to present your body with the same physical challenge all of the time it will eventually cease to give positive responses to the stagnant challenge. You must press onward and upward. The body wants to stay where it is or revert back to where you were when you started; you must force it to move ahead. You cannot become complacent about your training. If you stay with the same training program all of the time without moving ahead you will soon develop a training rut. The longer you stay in the rut the less productive your work-

Nasser El Sonbaty, Kevin Levrone and Shawn Ray

BODYBUILDING IS THE QUICKEST WAY TO MAKE SOME EXTREMELY POSITIVE CHANGES TO YOUR BODY.

outs will be. Your body will adapt to the current training and then cease to make any changes beyond that point. So you must present your body with progressive challenges to get positive changes.

Here is how the overload/progressive adaptation principle works in the gym. If you were to curl 60 pounds for some time your body would become used to that amount of weight. It would cease to respond beyond how it did in the initial stages, when you first curled the 60 pounds. To provoke further strength and size gains, you would need to give the body a new challenge. You can do this by increasing the amount of repetitions you curl with the 60 pounds. If you were curling this weight for 8 repetitions in the beginning stages, then an increase in the amount of repetitions would give the body a new challenge. However, you can use this method of increasing the repetition range only so far. The body gives diminishing returns after a certain repetition range. This seems to be around 12 to 15 repetitions for the upper body and 15 to 20 repetitions for the lower body. Beyond that range the response the body provides is minimal. So to continue to overload the body beyond that point you need to increase the amount of weight used. In the example used, after you have increased the curl repetition range to around 12 repetitions, you would then increase the amount of weight used to 70 pounds. When you increase the amount of weight for an exercise you cannot perform as many repetitions. The repetitions you can perform with the new and heavier weight decreases. When you increased the amount of weight to 70, perhaps your repetition range would drop to around 6. You would then continue to use the 70-pound weight until you could perform it for 12 repetitions. At this point you would again be at a lower repetition range and would repeat the entire cycle again. And it is a cycle. You stay with a weight for a period of time until you can use that weight for the maximum repetition range (12 to 15 for upper body; 15 to 20 for lower body) then you add weight and repeat the cycle. Certain parts of bodybuilding are quite basic and simple. The overload/ progressive adaptation principle is one area that is very basic. You learn it, then you keep using it over and over again.

WEIGHT TRAINING AND INCREMENTAL INCREASES

Another principle that goes hand in hand with the overload/pro- gressive adaptation principle is incremental training. You take advantage of the body's adapta- tion capability with incremental increases. This was mentioned in the section on overload/ positive adaptation. You incre- mentally increase the difficulty of your training (with a slight overload). This is what makes

Shawn Ray

weightlifting such an awesome tool to mold your body. The weights are balanced and can be equally added to each side of the bar (barbell or dumbell) or are already complete and you can simply use the next larger weight in the rack (a gym usually has a rack of weights in graduated poundages). Weight machines use the same principle – they are built to allow you to incrementally increase the difficulty of the training. You select a heavier weight on the stack of iron after you have mastered the previous weight. When you are using weight training to shape your body you can get quite precise in the incremental increase you choose to use. As a general rule, the incremental increase in barbell training is 10 pounds (for instance, increasing your bench press from 135 pounds to 145 pounds). For dumbells the incremental increase is 5 pounds (increasing a dumbell curl from 25 pounds to 30 pounds). Remember, however, that this is just a general guideline. Some people like to increase the weight more each time they "max" out at one weight, and others choose to go up less. There are 1 1/4-pound weights that can be added to a bar to provide a smaller incremental increase. You can even make your own or have someone else make them if you want a smaller weight for a smaller increase.

Incrementally increasing the weights gives you exact control over your training progress. The best manner in which to keep exact control over your training is to use a notebook. Many bodybuilders have found a notebook and pen to be a training advantage. Take the notebook to the gym and use it to keep track of the weight amounts, repetitions, and sets you use for each training session. You can also note extra items and insights you have to help each new workout be better than the previous one. That is the aim of incremental training – to make each workout progressively more challenging than the last. If you do happen to miss some workouts due to illness, a vacation, work, etc., you can check your notebook to find out what your previous progress was, then work back up to that level of incremental increases. A training notebook (also called a training diary) allows you to keep track of past workouts and what your strength levels were at specific times in the past. This lets you know if you have been making gains in your training during any given time period (provided you are dating your workouts).

REST AND RECUPERATION

Incremental training is tough training. Overloading the body on a regular basis puts a certain stress level on it. It is very important to get adequate rest. The rule to remember is that the body grows during rest periods. And it grows most during sleep. You cannot continue to hammer at the body's reserve without giving the body adequate time to recover. When you work out you tear down the muscles as well as drain the body's

Training Tip: Keep a notebook (a training diary) for your workouts. This will allow your training to be more precise.

Vince Taylor and
Shawn Ray

reserve stores. It is necessary to give the body time to repair itself before you attack it again. Continual neglect of this principle will cause your body to go into a state of "overtraining" where any additional training will make the body begin to lose the gains it has accumulated. Overtraining wrecks the body. The body needs 48 hours of rest between the same type of workout routines. For example, if you work your chest on Monday, you shouldn't exercise the chest again until at least Thursday. You could work a different bodypart on the next day (training the legs on Tuesday, for instance, would be fine) but you must give the body a minimum of 48 hours between workouts of the same muscle group. The shaping of the body – adding muscularity and getting rid of fat, is a combined effort. One of the key elements is rest and recuperation. You cannot afford to neglect this area and expect to make any significant training gains. You need to pay as much attention to proper recuperation as you do to other aspects of training.

INTENSITY

Rest and recuperation are very important when you are away from the gym and your training. However, they are the exact opposite of what you need in the gym. A key principle for bringing about positive physical change is intensity. Intensity is the combination of concentration and superhard effort focused on an exercise routine. As **Mike Mentzer**, superstar bodybuilder and trainer, points out, "The corner-stone principle

> **YOU NEED TO PAY AS MUCH ATTENTION TO PROPER RECUPERATION AS YOU DO TO OTHER ASPECTS OF TRAINING.**

Craig Titus and Ericca Kern

The Fundamentals of Shaping Your Physique

Mike Mentzer

of the science of productive bodybuilding exercise is intensity . . . properly defined, it refers to the percentage of possible momentary muscular effort being exerted. A healthy, well-conditioned bodybuilder is capable of exerting 100 percent of his possible momentary muscular ability at practically any time. It is only on the last rep of a set carried to the point of momentary muscular failure, however, that one is forced to exert 100 percent of his momentary ability. Such an all-out effort is the single most important factor responsible for inducing muscular growth beyond normal levels in human beings."[5]

As you can deduce from that statement, ambivalent training will produce ambivalent results. Training must be focused. Training must be hard. Your body has it quite easy outside of the gym, but in the gym you have to go hard. A good motto is "go hard or go home." It takes a supreme effort to mold muscles, to force size and shape out of the reluctant human physique. You have to battle metal for mastery. You have to break through the "pain barrier."

The "pain barrier" is a phenomenon in physique training that is somewhat similar to the runner's mile. It is an unseen obstacle which really hurts. However, it rewards the person who pushes past it with more rapid muscle growth. The pain barrier is the place in training where the exercise becomes very difficult. For example, if you were curling 70 pounds, the first five repetitions may cause the muscles to burn with a bit of pain. After the sixth and seventh repetitions you feel you cannot go on any further. But you reach down deep inside and force up two more repetitions, pushing past the pain and pulling the bar up with everything you have. You have just pushed past the pain barrier. What happens then? It is when you get past the pain barrier that you really start to make progress in bodybuilding. Busting past the pain barrier into the rapid growth zone is difficult but it pays big dividends.

Pushing past the pain barrier is something you should not really get into until you have a few months of initial training under your belt. You need some time to get familiar with "good" pain and "bad" pain. Good pain is pain that comes as a result of challenging the muscles to step up to a new level of development. Bad pain is pain that occurs because you are doing something incorrectly. You do need to handle pain. It was from bodybuilding that the phrase "no pain, no gain" gained its popularity. What it means is that if you are not intense in your training, if you do not push yourself until you hurt, your results will be minimal. It takes real intense training, training that challenges the muscles until they hurt, to move ahead. However, this pain is muscle pain. It is not to be confused with joint pain, or bone pain. The good pain is the pain your muscles feel as a result of lifting heavier weights or jogging further than before. After a few months of working out you will become familiar with this pain and then you will be able to distinguish between "good" pain and "bad" pain. Once you have that knowledge down, you can move on to breaking through the pain barrier for awesome results.

MUSCLE PAIN

In addition to the pain you feel during the final repetitions of an exercise, there will also be some pain within the next couple of days. The delayed pain is also a result of your workout. If you don't know this it can come as quite a shock. The pain will be present in the muscles you have worked in the previous workout. The pain lets you know your workouts have been effective, and it also lets you know exactly where your training hit home. Sometimes you realize from the delayed pain that the exercise you were using to target an area got another muscle group. Muscle pain gives you great feedback on your workout.

Bill Pearl

You can alleviate much of the pain by stretching before, during, and after the workout. Some bodybuilders have also found that swimming after working out is a great way to prevent the pain from becoming as evident.

Although the concept of muscle pain sounds nasty, once you begin training you will soon become accustomed to it and will hardly notice it after you have a few months of training under your belt.

VARIETY - CYCLED INTENSITY

As important as intensity is, you do not always want to go at the weights with 100 percent superintensity. A break every now and then with some lighter weights is an approach that many professionals use. Training variety is very important. Five-time Mr. Universe **Bill Pearl** points out that he puts a great deal of importance on variety.[6] This variety can be in

The Fundamentals of Shaping Your Physique

the type of exercises, and in the manner they are used – the intensity. For the most part training should be superintense, but you can take a period of time to train less intensely.

MUSCLE MEMORY

Another factor in training the physique is "muscle memory." It has been said that the human mind, once stretched by a new idea, never goes back to the former manner of lesser thinking. The principle of muscle memory is somewhat similar to that thought, except it is applied to the body. Muscle, when not used, does shrink back toward its original untrained state, but it never goes all of the way back. It retains what has been tagged "muscle memory." That is, the muscle remembers its previous training and responds quickly to renewed training. For instance, if one person who was new to working out was trying to reach a 300-pound bench press and started training with a partner who had not been training for awhile but had benched 300 pounds in the past, the person who had bench pressed 300 pounds in the past would achieve the current 300-pound bench press twice as fast as the person who had never done it before. The muscles seem to retain some inner spark, gaining the ability to spring back to the level they had formerly attained fairly quickly. This is a positive factor. It can help you return to previous training levels after having to spend some time away from training (due to illness, business, etc.).

> **Super Training Tip:** To alleviate muscle pain after a workout, spend a few minutes stretching the area that hurts. If possible, get in some easy swimming.

Lou Ferrigno, Serge Nubret and Arnold Schwarzenegger

In that same line of thought an old myth can be dispelled. Muscles do not turn to fat when you quit training. This myth (that muscles turn into fat) has no factual basis. Muscle tissue and fat tissue are two different things altogether. It would be similar to stating that fat can turn into bone. It is an impossibility. Muscle and fat are like apples and oranges – you cannot compare the two. If you continue to eat at the level you were eating at when you worked out you could get fat when you quit training, but this would only be because of the high level of caloric intake as opposed to a lesser level of burning off calories. Muscles do not turn into fat when they are not used, they simply get smaller (atrophy). When you work on them again they quickly spring back to a bigger size.

INSTINCTIVE TRAINING

It is very important to learn the basic fundamentals of building your body through the sport and art form of bodybuilding. These proven principles will guide you to the muscle growth that you want to achieve. Use of the principles will save you a lot of wasted time and frustration trying to find out what will and won't work for a workout. Go with the suggested guide-

Flex Wheeler and Paul Dillett

28   MUSCLE BUILDING 101

Darry Thornton

lines for shaping your physique. However, once you have gotten a good grasp of the fundamental basics for building your body, you can then experiment to some degree. The experimentation should be directed toward what will work for your body. This is called "instinctive training." You may come to the gym some day and find that your normal workout is not providing you with the response that you want, so you try something new. You become an "Edison" in the gym. You may find that you get a better response on some exercise by slightly twisting your wrist as you complete the exercise. Or you may find that you get a better response on another exercise by performing it at a different angle. It is through "instinctive training" that you custom-tailor your workout to meet the precise needs of your unique physique. **Paul Dillett,** a massive bodybuilder, uses instinctive training quite often. For example, he says, "Every time I train my biceps, the workout will be different." [7] Many bodybuilders vary their training on various bodyparts. However, remember that instinctive training should be the exception rather than the rule for most workouts in the beginning and intermediate stages. Stay more with the basics, especially in the beginning stages of your training.

BODYBUILDING, POWERLIFTING AND OLYMPIC WEIGHTLIFTING

There are three basic types of weight training – bodybuilding, power-lifting, and Olympic weightlifting. Powerlifting and Olympic weightlifting focus almost entirely on lifting weights whereas bodybuilding is more broad in nature and incorporates other activities.

Powerlifting is a sport involving three movements – the squat, the bench press, and the deadlift. The goal is to lift as heavy a weight as possible in each of these exercises, then the amount from each is totaled and a winner declared. The competitive classes are divided out by body-weight size. Powerlifters are very strong in each of these three exercises. Powerlifters are the strongest of all those who lift weights.

Olympic weightlifting is an Olympic sport which involves lifting weights in two exercises, the snatch and the clean and jerk. The goal is to be able to win the sport by lifting the most weight in these movements. Olympic weightlifting is as much technique as it is strength. The Olympic weightlifters are very strong in the two exercises that they perform.

Bodybuilding is a sport that focuses on the physique rather than on the weights. Weights are one tool for shaping the body, but weights are not the sole focus as with the other two weightlifting sports. The shape of the physique is the main aim for bodybuilding training. A powerlifter or Olympic weightlifter may be very strong, but also may be somewhat fat.

> MUSCLES DO NOT TURN INTO FAT WHEN THEY ARE NOT USED, THEY SIMPLY GET SMALLER.

Since neither of these sports are very concerned about the appearance of the body, they do not worry as much if they are fat. But to a bodybuilder fat is a dreaded enemy. In addition to being strong, a bodybuilder wants to look fantastic. A power-lifter or Olympic weightlifter may be strong or have large muscles in a couple of areas on the body; but a bodybuilder works on every area of the body to ensure that every muscle group is strong, well-developed, and looks great. A bodybuilder is concerned about body balance, muscle symmetry, and the lines of the muscles. Bodybuilders generally build specific muscle groups up much larger than the other two weightlifting sports. For instance, a powerlifter or Olympic lifter, while quite strong, may have fairly small arms. A bodybuilder will have tremen-dous arm size. And a powerlifter or Olympic weightlifter may have a large stomach, while a bodybuilder is typified by a very small waistline. Since one of the main aims of a bodybuilder is to have a very low percentage of bodyfat combined with large muscle development, a bodybuilder has a body that

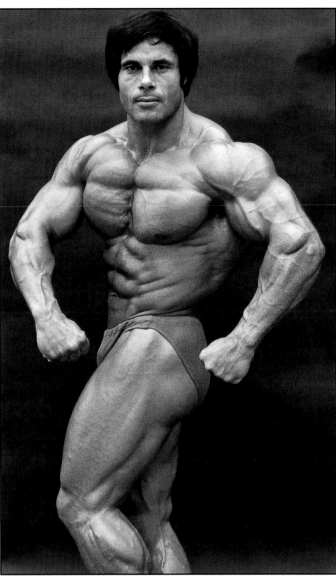

Franco Columbu

looks a lot better than a powerlifter or an Olympic lifter. There are a few rare exceptions as some powerlifters or Olympic lifters also include some bodybuilding training in their routine. And the reverse is also true – many bodybuilders include some powerlifting movements and occasion-ally an Olympic lift to increase their overall body power and strength. **Lee Haney,** Mr. Olympia for eight consecutive years, points to powerlifting as a key ingredient in his bodybuilding training. **Franco Columbu** was a bodybuilder who used powerlifting quite extensively and built a tremen-dously strong physique. Massive **Mike Francois** started as an Olympic-style lifter and credits his incredible upper-arm development to some of his Olympic lifting training. [8]

Most people find that bodybuilding is the best of the three sports for achieving their personal physique goals. Many aspects of bodybuilding have been incorporated into many different sports over the past few decades (for example, boxing, football, tennis, etc.) to assist the athlete in becoming stronger, larger, quicker, and more balanced. Bodybuilding has been the most dynamic sport of the last half of this century.

The Fundamentals of Shaping Your Physique

There are two basic levels of bodybuilding – competitive bodybuilding and personal bodybuilding. Competitive bodybuilding is a sport that involves presenting your physique in a variety of poses before a panel of judges who determine the best physique. The winner gets a title such as "Mr. Universe," "Mr. World," etc. The top title is "Mr. Olympia." There are amateur and professional levels of competitive bodybuilding, and the professional bodybuilders get paid for winning the various titles. They also earn endorsement money from various companies involved in fitness products. Some of the top bodybuilders make a fairly good living at the sport. Competitive bodybuilding comprises a very small percentage of those involved in the sport of bodybuilding. Of all those involved in bodybuilding, perhaps five to 10 percent or less are involved in competitive bodybuilding. Most people are into personal bodybuilding.

Michael Francois

Personal bodybuilding involves using bodybuilding to fashion the physique that you want. For instance, if your arms are too small and your waist is too large, bodybuilding is the best way to handle the problem. If you have too much bodyfat, the quickest manner in which to change this nasty physique predicament is to use bodybuilding techniques to bring about rapid change. If your legs are too thin, or your chest is too small, consistent bodybuilding will change your body. Personal bodybuilding is the quickest manner in which to positively change your physique! As more and more people are discovering, bodybuilding is a fantastic tool to shape the physique – adding size where necessary, and getting rid of bodyfat. You don't have to get into competitive bodybuilding to enjoy tremendous benefits from bodybuilding. You can use personal bodybuilding to build up your physique into fantastic shape. You can add more lean muscle, get rid of bodyfat, and shape your body into a "hot" appearance that really turns heads. Bodybuilding is also a great tool for fighting the effects of aging. A person who engages in bodybuilding can maintain a superhot physique well into his or her latter years and enjoy those latter years more. **Bill Pearl,** former unbeaten Mr. Universe, is 65 and still going strong, thanks to bodybuilding. His physique is that of a 40-year-old man. Bodybuilding is truly an awesome sport to be engaged in and personal bodybuilding allows anyone who wants to be involved to participate at the level that he or she chooses. The great thing about personal bodybuilding is that it allows you to determine exactly what you want to do with your body, and then do it. You don't have a coach telling you what he or she wants, and you don't have a boss or neighbor making a decision on what is best for you. You get to do what you want with your body. Personal bodybuilding is perhaps the most independent form of sporting involvement that exists. Once you know the basic principles you can use them to do whatever you want with your physique.

TRAINING TERMINOLOGY

There are certain terms that will be used again and again in the sport of bodybuilding. Knowing what they are will help you more readily understand the sport of bodybuilding. You may know some of the terms; others may be new to you. Get a good grasp of each before beginning to train.

Exercise – An exercise is a specific fitness activity that you engage in for a specific result. For instance, a pushup is an exercise. So is a dumbell curl. Exercises can be aerobic/cardiovascular in nature (running), or anaerobic in nature (weightlifting). Exercises have specific functions and give certain results. Some exercises, for example, work the legs; others work the upper body.

> ONCE YOU KNOW THE BASIC PRINCIPLES YOU CAN USE THEM TO DO WHATEVER YOU WANT WITH YOUR PHYSIQUE.

**Rich Gaspari,
Lee Haney and
Lee Labrada**

Incorporate cardiovascular workouts into your training since they are the quickest and most proven manner in which to burn bodyfat.
– Lee Apperson

Aerobic/Cardiovascular – Exercises that demand a big oxygen uptake are called "aerobic/cardiovascular" exercises. These exercises are continuous in nature and stimulate the heart, lungs, and other body systems. They generally provide minimal muscle-building benefits beyond an initial surge, but they do provide an excellent way to condition the heart and lungs. They also get rid of bodyfat. Aerobic/cardiovascular work builds endurance and stamina. For aerobic/cardiovascular work to be effective, it should last for at least 20 minutes of nonstop activity. This is just about the point where the body starts to burn off fat. The best aerobic/cardiovascular effects occur when you take your heart into the 60 to 70 percent of maximum heart beat range. The combination of burning off fat and increasing your endurance is great for building a better looking and more healthy body. Some of the more popular aerobic/cardiovascular exercises include jogging, swimming, biking or stationary biking, Nordic skiing or Nordic track skiing, rowing, aerobics, stair-stepping, power walking, treadmill walking, jumping rope, and several other similar activities. Once you work up to a base of a minimum of 20 minutes of nonstop aerobic/cardio work, increase the time you spend on these activities to 30 minutes, with an occasional 45+ minute session. The sport of bodybuilding does not go overboard on aerobic/cardio work because too much focus on these activities can cut into the other areas; specifically, too much aerobic/cardiovascular work can slow down muscle-size gains. You only have so much energy output potential and it needs to be balanced between aerobic/cardio exercises and anaerobic exercises. For the most effective bodybuilding results, more emphasis needs to be put on the anaerobic (weight training) exercises. However, do not make the mistake of neglecting aerobic/cardiovascular workouts since they are the quickest and most proven manner in which to burn off bodyfat, one of the main objectives of bodybuilding. To be effective, aerobic/cardio work should be performed at least 2 or 3 times a week.

Anaerobic/Muscular Exercise – Anaerobic/muscular exercise is a type of exercise that does not require long nonstop repetitive actions like running, but rather short bursts of powerful outputs of energy. Instead of a sustained effort, you perform a brief, intense, specific action. Weight training is anaerobic in nature. You could not continuously lift a weight nonstop for twenty minutes, especially if it were really heavy. Weight training is designed to be a maximal burst of all-out energy focused on moving a weight in a specified pattern. Intensity plays a big part in weight training. Nonintense workouts produce minimal, if any, results. Just going through the motions won't build up muscles. To be effective, anaerobic training has to be intense.

Paul Dillett

Anaerobic training is also most effective when it is progressive. When you use aerobic/cardiovascular training you tend to work up to a point where you plateau and then stay at that point. For instance, you may work up to a 40-minute run, and then stay at that level for quite some time. But with anaerobic training you should always be striving to surge ahead. As mentioned earlier in the section on progressive adaptation and the principle of incremental increases, your body will give you some positive muscle response in the initial stages of using a certain weight, but will cease to respond after a period of time. The crucial factor is to increase the difficulty of the anaerobic exercise – putting more weight on the bar. The principles of anaerobic training are particularly suited to weight training. You can use weight training for aerobic/cardiovascular work by employing a circuit approach (rushing from one weightlifting exercise to another without any rest for 15 to 30 minutes) but the muscle-building effects of circuit training are minimal when compared to regular weight training where you take a rest between sets (sets and repetitions will be defined in the following pages).

How long of a rest should you take between sets? Generally, just enough to catch your breath. The body returns to almost full energy capacity within 35 to 60 seconds. A minute to two-minute rest between sets is about perfect for most weight workouts. Sometimes when your objectives are different you may use a shorter or longer rest between sets. For instance, if you are lifting some maximum low-repetition poundages you will perform better if you rest longer between sets. If you are trying to force a pump you can get a better result with a shorter rest between sets. Your body may respond somewhat differently so it would be wise to listen to your body and use a little "instinctive training" to figure out exactly what the best rest period between sets would be for your physique.

Anaerobic training is a powerful manner in which to change the shape of the physique – particularly the size and shape of the muscles. Weight training is the primary style of anaerobic exercise.

The Fundamentals of Shaping Your Physique

Repetitions – A repetition is a fundamental term for bodybuilding purposes. A repetition is one full motion of any exercise. For instance, if you take a barbell and curl it upward from the thigh level to the level of the chin, then lower it to thigh level again, this would be one repetition of the curl exercise. The same holds true for nonweightlifting exercises. If you are in the up position for the pushup exercise (prone, arms extended) and lower yourself to the ground, then come back up again, you have just performed one repetition of the pushup. A repetition is one full motion of an exercise.

A repetition should be performed in a full and complete motion, with movement from the top of the position to the bottom (or vice versa, depending upon where the motion for that particular exercise starts) in a smooth groove. Jerky, rushed motions can lead to injuries. An incomplete repetition can lead to incomplete muscle development. As was mentioned earlier, the number of repetitions you perform has a specific effect upon the body. Researchers have found that in general 1 to 5 repetitions will build strength and power; 6 to 15 repetitions will build muscle size; and beyond that repetitions build endurance.[9] Those are generally the repetition ranges that most bodybuilders rely on. Power-lifters tend to use repetition ranges from 1 to 5; bodybuilders usually use 6 to 15 repetitions. This number is not an absolute – sometimes a bodybuilder will spend some time building power into his body and use a lower repetition range, or sometimes the muscles are shocked with a higher repetition range. Another general rule of thumb is to use higher repetitions for the legs than for the upper body. A general repetition

Roland Kickinger

range for the upper body might be from 6 to 15 repetitions; a general range for the legs would be from 8 to 20 repetitions. Some bodybuilders mix the repetition ranges during a workout session and perform some exercises at a lower range and an exercise for the same bodypart at a higher repetition range. There is room for a lot of experimentation with repetition ranges so discover your best range through trial and error. Aim at the repetition range that best suits your objectives – strength, size, or endurance. And remember to increase the amount of weight that you are using when you can handle the exercise for the maximum amount of repetitions in the range you want to work within.

Sets – Closely tied into the definition of repetitions is the term "sets." A set is a group of repetitions performed nonstop. If you were to perform ten pushups and then stand up and rest, you would have performed one set of pushups. If you were to press a barbell over your head twelve times nonstop, that would be considered one set of barbell presses. A set can consist of as many repetitions as you choose. A set may consist of only one repetition, or it may consist of twenty repetitions. The key is that a set is a united effort of nonstop repetitions for one exercise. Sets are grouped together to work a muscle group with a certain type of exercise. If you were working the chest, you might perform bench presses for 3 sets of 8 repetitions. If you were working the legs, you might perform 4 sets of 10 repetitions of the squat exercise. Generally, you perform a few sets for each exercise. The amount of sets you perform for each exercise varies, but usually falls into a range of 2 to 5. A set should be performed with maximum intensity throughout all repetitions; in fact the last repetitions of a set should be the most intense.

> **A REPETITION IS ONE FULL MOTION OF ANY SPECIFIC EXERCISE.**

Shawn Ray, Vince Taylor and Kevin Levrone

The late
Vince Gironda

The Workout – Several exercises performed for several sets of several repetitions comprise a workout. A workout is a group of exercises that are performed one after another, each with a few sets of several repetitions. An exercise may be a full-body workout (exercises for all of the major muscle groups) or it may be focused on one area of the body (upper body or lower body.). You can plan your workout schedule in any manner you choose; however, it is best to use suggested workouts in the beginning stages of bodybuilding. It is important to remember the rule of giving each major muscle group at least 48 hours of rest between workouts when you are setting up your workout schedules. Another name for the workout is "routine." Sometimes people mean workout when they use the generic term exercise (as opposed to the term "specific exercise"), as in "I'm going to go exercise." A workout may last anywhere from 15 minutes to over an hour. The most effective workout time period for building muscle size and strength, according to empirical evidence, seems to be about 45 minutes. After that point testosterone and energy levels dip downward. The ultimate iron guru, **Vince Gironda,** advocates a 45-minute workout. It is important not to make a workout last too long. A workout that lasts too long wreaks havoc with your recuperative powers and tends to push you toward an "overtrained" state where muscle mass is lost. Several workout programs will be provided in upcoming chapters of *Muscle Building 101.*

Muscle Groups – There are hundreds of different muscles in the human body. The bodybuilding program focuses on training the muscles by major groupings. When training the body there are just a few major muscle groups that are concentrated on. These include: chest, back, shoulders, biceps, triceps, and legs. The minor groupings focused on are the neck, waist, and forearms. Sometimes the major groups are divided up into smaller subgroups. For instance, a chest workout might focus on exercising the upper, inner, and outer chest. Shoulder-training may be broken into deltoid- and trapezius-training. The best manner in which to build the body is with a concentrated focus on the major muscle groups. This concentration of effort allows the muscle group to be intensely trained to the point where it has to respond. The pump effect is also used. A major muscle group should be worked with another major muscle group that is contiguous so that the blood that rushes into the first group is nearby and available for the second group. That is why it is better to work shoulders with the chest than with the legs.

As you work with them, you will become more familiar with the major muscle groups and how they respond to different types of training.

The Pump – The "pump" is a phenomenon that originated in bodybuilding. The "pump" is the terminology given to the feeling that occurs when the blood rushes into a muscle group. When several repetitions of concentrated exercise have been performed on a muscle group it "pumps" up with blood, much like a balloon pumps up with air. This engorgement of the muscles makes it significantly larger than it was

GENERAL REPETITION RULE OF THUMB:
1-5 REPS = STRENGTH
6-15 REPS = SIZE
15+ REPS = ENDURANCE

prior to the workout. This "pump" lasts for about 30 minutes after the workout and serves as a positive effect – it nourishes the muscle with high-octane blood while removing unwanted waste from the system. Some bodybuilders swear that the pump is necessary to build big muscles. **Arnold Schwarzenegger** believed the pump to be the ultimate sensation. Once you have pumped up a muscle you will come to know the unmistakable feeling of being "pumped up."

Cycles – A cycle is a series of workouts aimed at a specific end. You may want to put on some more body size, and have a training cycle devoted totally to that endeavor. A cycle is generally progressive in nature, culminating in the achievement of a specific short-term goal or advancement toward a long-term goal. For example, you may want to place primary focus on training your legs. You might employ a leg "cycle," where you train in a concentrated manner, concentrating on just your legs. After you achieve your objectives, you would move on to another type of cycle. A cycle generally lasts anywhere from a few weeks up to half a year in length. There are hundreds of types of cycles – cycles for size, strength, specific bodyparts (arm cycle, etc.). Some bodybuilders use a two-part cycle during the year – building body size in one part of the year, and building body shape in another part of the year. Some bodybuilders don't use any cycles at all; they prefer to use the same training system all of the time. Several different cycle options will be presented and explained later in the book.

Supersets, Trisets, and Giant Sets – The concept of the "set" has already been presented. There are advanced uses of the set in body-building which include supersets, trisets, and giant sets. The superset is two sets of different exercises performed back-to-back without rest until both sets are completed. For instance, if you were to use a superset on the chest, you would perhaps perform a set of bench presses followed by a set of pushups without resting between either exercise. You would rest *after* the pair of sets were finished. A triset is three sets performed nonstop, and a giant set is four sets performed nonstop. The aim of

Start

The Fundamentals of Shaping Your Physique

these multiple sets is to get a super pump in a very short period of time. They are advanced techniques and generally the body does not work well with them until the advanced stages of training. Bodybuilding in the basic stages does not need to be concerned with all of the multiset workouts.

Barbells – A barbell is a long bar with balanced weights attached to either end. The barbells of yesteryear were fixed in nature; the modern barbells are adjustable. You can add weight to both ends to increase the amount of the barbell or take weights off to decrease the amount of the barbell. There are two basic types of barbells currently used – the standard and the Olympic. The standard barbell is the same thickness throughout the length of the bar; the Olympic barbell has a thicker end-piece on either end and takes a weight plate with larger holes. The Olympic barbell is generally the better made of the two.

Some barbells have a knurled area for a better grip and a floating sleeve that allows the center of the bar to remain stationary as the weights shift.

Finish

Barbell plates vary in size, from the very small to the huge (1 1/4 pounds to 100 pounds). The weight plates for barbells move in general increments of 2 1/2 to 5 to 10 pounds for the lighter plates, and increase more rapidly past the 25-pound plate. The Olympic barbell has a common 45-pound plate. The barbells are capped with a collar which tightens down after the desired weight is placed on the bar. It is important to get the weight evenly balanced to avoid an injury while lifting.

Barbells are generally used for lifting heavier amounts. Barbells require the use of both hands and are best for compound movements.

Compound and Isolation Movements – Compound movements are lifts involving more than one major muscle group. For instance, bench presses utilize the back, chest, shoulders, and triceps. Compound movements involve the use of a primary muscle group and one or more secondary muscle groups. For bench presses, the chest is the primary muscle group, and the other muscle groups are secondary. The compound movements promote strength and muscle mass.

Isolation movements focus totally on a single muscle group to the exclusion of all others. Isolation movements work great for shaping a muscle. Dumbell exercises work best for isolation movements.

Barbells come in a variety of styles. Danny Hester reps out on reverse-grip curls with a standard EZ-curl barbell.

Dumbells – Dumbells are smaller weights that fit into each hand. A dumbell may be either fixed or adjustable. Although a dumbell is smaller, they can still be quite heavy. A range of dumbells may be from 5 pounds to 150 pounds in increments of 5 pounds. A new style of dumbell has recently come on the market – an adjustable dumbell stand where you simply move a switch to activate the size of dumbell you want to use. This type of dumbell is probably the wave of the future.

Finish

Start

A dumbell is ideal for isolation work because it focuses on a single muscle group. An example of this would be the dumbell concentration curl. The only muscle really involved is the biceps. Dumbells are great for a fine focus on specific muscles. Dumbells also work great on hitting the muscles from different angles. With a dumbell you can turn the wrist at different angles and get a different response dependent upon the angle. You can't do that with a barbell.

Dumbells and barbells have different functions and both are important tools for building a great body.

Dumbells can give you the muscle isolation you desire. Jean-Pierre Fux "pumps" his biceps with dumbell concentration curls.

Weight Machines – There are a variety of different weight-training machines available for building the body. Most of the machines on the market work great, and there always seems to be a "new and improved" version available. Machines work in much the same manner for adding weight, with incrementally heavier selections. Weight machines are nice because you don't need a partner to "spot" you as you lift, so you can go as heavy as you want. The one big drawback is that machines take away the "balance" factor, a key component in shaping the muscles. Free-weight training (barbells and dumbells) is the ultimate manner in which to train but the machines keep getting better. In fact, for some exercises, a machine works better than free weights. If you work out at a gym that has machines, mix them in with your training but don't totally rely on them. Free-weight training is still the best way to build the body for most exercises.

The Spotter – A spotter is a person who is available to assist you with a heavy weight so you don't injure yourself. For example, if you are going to attempt to lift a very heavy weight in the bench press or squat, you might need some help if you fail to get the weight up. A spotter stands over you and makes certain you get the weight back to the starting point in the event that your strength runs out. If you need an occasional "spot" from someone else you should be willing to "spot" them also. This type of assistance is usually only necessary when you are working with very heavy poundages.

Bodybuilding is the ultimate manner in which to shape the physique. No other sport or activity brings about a more rapid transformation of the human physique. If you want to change the way you look, bodybuilding is the best sport to choose.

References

1. Reg Bradford, "The Dorian Yates Seminar," *Muscular Development* (February 1996), 127.
2. Greg Zulak, "Aussie Delts," *MuscleMag International* (October 1993), 22.
3. Overheard, *MuscleMag International* (June 1994), 251.
4. Bobby Douglas, *Take it to the Mat,* (Ames, Iowa: Sigler Printing & Publishing, 1993), xii.
5. Mike Mentzer, "On Overtraining," *Muscular Development* (February 1996), 46.
6. Bill Pearl & David Prokop, "20 months to a Champion Physique," *Ironman* (October 1994), 46.
7. Paul Dillett, "24 Inches of Monster Meat," *Flex* (August 1992), 136.
8. Mike Francois and Jerry Brainum, "Ungodly Guns," *Flex* (January 1996), 53.
9. Charles Poliquin, "The Science of Reps," *Muscle Media 2000* (July 1995), 88-89.

> **IF YOU WANT TO CHANGE THE WAY YOU LOOK, BODYBUILDING IS THE BEST SPORT TO CHOOSE.**

Have a spotter assist you with heavy poundages so you don't injure yourself. A spotter can also provide the motivation you need to squeeze out one last rep.

THE MASSIVE POWER OF THE MIND

When you think of bodybuilding, or any other sport, you think primarily about the body. And rightly so – building the body is about the body. But what most people don't know is that the most awesome part of the body is the mind. Both work together. **Mike Mentzer** writes, "The idea of a healthy mind in a healthy body comes to us from the age of classical Greece, 23 centuries ago."[1] The mind is the key to building the body. The mind makes the body perform in the manner that the mind commands the body to do so.

Mike Mentzer

The mind is very powerful. Think about this – what put mankind on the moon? It was the mind of man. Man, who had stared up at the moon for thousands of years, devised a mode to reach the moon. The power of the mind is literally awesome. **Berry DeMey,** professional bodybuilder, stated that "the mind is a powerful tool."[2] That power can work for you in training your physique. You can channel this awesome power in the gym and take your physique to new levels. The correct use of the mind is the key to bodybuilding success. **Arnold Schwarzenegger** points out the power of the mind in building the body in his books.

There are several traits of the mind that can be developed just as the body is developed. These traits act as the driving force behind the necessary workouts to take the body to higher levels of development.

Discipline

One of the most potent factors of all in any type of training is discipline. The first step of a military training program or a football program is to install discipline into the troops or

Bruce Patterson

THE MIND IS
THE KEY
TO BUILDING
THE BODY.

team. Discipline is crucial to achieving success in any given endeavor. This is particularly true for bodybuilding. However, with bodybuilding, the discipline does not come for a coach or drill instructor. It must come from within. A statement on discipline that really is pertinent appeared in a college newspaper: "The undisciplined is a headache to himself and a heartache to others, and is unprepared to face the stern realities of life."[3]

Perhaps what could also be stated is that the undisciplined is unprepared to face the stern realities of the gym. You have to earn, to build and develop, a fantastic physique. Discipline is crucial. The development of personal discipline is a critical determining factor for whether or not you will succeed in building a better body. Nobody has it easy. Champions hurt in the gym, too. **Bruce Patterson** relates that he would train from three o'clock until 6:30 in the evening and "train his guts out."[4] Big **Gary Strydom** says, "I admit I don't particularly enjoy leg-training. I love to bomb my arms, chest, back, and delts, but I hate the pain associated with heavy leg workouts."[5] Note that the discipline must be personal. You have to make your body get up and go to the gym. You have to make your body lift the heavier weight, and you have to make your body attempt that last painful repetition. Discipline must become so much a part of you that it is an automatic response. That is what the military and sports training programs strive for – to build automatic discipline. It is part of what bodybuilding is all about – choosing the harder path for the greater reward. Discipline produces delayed gratification. You put off a smaller enjoyment today in place of a greater enjoyment later. You choose not to spend the evening on the sofa watching football (the smaller reward); instead you choose to go to the gym and work out. Pain is often involved in discipline. Lifting weights is painful, especially the last few repetitions. A strongly disciplined mind keeps you focused on your goal through the pain. Discipline and pain are often closely related. **Tom Platz,** the man with "unreal" leg development, says, "Physically, I don't finish a set until I literally can't work the fatigued muscle any longer. I more or less continue a set until the bar literally drops from my momentarily paralyzed fingers."[6] That's discipline in the face of pain!

Discipline must also be utilized in order to get your workout done despite outside distractions. One writer observed that the great **Sergio Oliva** had an appointment to make, but Sergio would not let the appointment interfere with his workout.[7] Discipline means that the workout comes first.

Gary Strydom

How do you build up discipline? You do so by setting goals and then systematically going after each goal until you achieve it. Another primary factor is motivation. Motivation is a key to becoming disciplined.

Motivation

Motivation is fuel for the mind, the desire that draws you toward what you want. If you really want something you will do just about whatever it takes to reach it. Motivation is one of life's more powerful elements. A wise bodybuilder learns to use motivation as a tool to reach his or her goals. Motivation is mental hunger, a hunger to have what you want. It is an inner appetite that won't be quenched until its reward is tasted. Famed **John Grimek** says, "When I was training for a major event, my ambition was keen and strong."[8] That is the key to making your workouts continue at a high level – ambition, and strong desire. If you want to build a better body badly enough you will have sufficient fuel for doing just that. Motivation makes discipline easy. Once you are motivated to achieve a goal, you simply keep at it until you reach it. Without motivation, discipline is really tough. So whatever goals you want from bodybuilding (more muscular bodyweight, bigger arms, a smaller waist, less bodyfat, etc.), make them crystal clear so that your motivation makes discipline logical and easy.

Goals and Plans

To have motivation and discipline you must have something to be motivated about and something to be disciplined for. That is where goals fit in. Your goals are targets that you shoot for in your training. Goals should always be set a little out of reach so that you put out maximum

> THE UNDISCIPLINED IS A HEADACHE TO HIMSELF AND A HEARTACHE TO OTHERS, AND IS UNPREPARED TO FACE THE STERN REALITIES OF LIFE.

effort in striving to reach them. Perhaps you want to bench press 200 pounds but are somewhat uncertain if you can reach that weight. Make it a goal and give it everything you have to reach it. Goals clarify training. If you have a goal, you have a path for your progress to proceed on. Without some type of goal a training program tends to flounder in the shallow waters of minimal gains. To make the most progress, set goals in every area of your training – body size, bodyfat percentage, amount of weight lifted per exercise, etc. These goals act as an incentive to continually move ahead. You can set smaller goals (increasing your curl weight by 25 pounds in the coming year) and larger goals (increasing your arm size by 2 inches within the next two years). The smaller goals can act as steps to the larger goals. Reaching a smaller goal builds your confidence.

Long-range plans are also essential. These type of goals involve the way you want your body to look in the long run. Long-range plans are extremely helpful in making your dreams a reality. **Lee Labrada,** one of the best built and knowledgeable bodybuilders of all time says that "there are mental aspects involved for guys to make it in the long run. . . . I think what it boils down to is that you have to have a long-range plan."[9] Set up short-term goals and long-range plans. Put them down on paper to hold yourself accountable.

Tom Platz

Confidence and Positive Attitude

Confidence is a trait that will flow from within as you begin to develop your physique. Former US Olympic wrestling coach **Bobby Douglas** noted that "you can use your strength training program to increase your personal confidence, that deep-down residue of inner belief that allows ordinary people to achieve extraordinary accomplishments in every area of life."[10] As you become stronger and more muscular, your confidence will soar to new heights. Your confidence will have a snowball effect – it will grow larger and larger as you continue to bodybuild. Mr. Olympia **Dorian Yates** noted in an interview before his first Olympia victory that "I'm gonna win the bloody thing!"[11] Dorian then went on to win that Olympia and the next four straight.

Another factor closely related to confidence is a positive attitude. You have to believe in yourself and your bodybuilding training. You have to avoid the negative attitude that holds so many people back from becoming all that they could be. The mind and body are closely in tune to each other and the body picks up on the mind's attitude. Some doctors estimate that around half the people in many hospitals are there because of psychosomatic disorders – problems of the body caused or initiated by the mind. Your mind is a powerful tool and that can work in either a positive or negative direction. You can build yourself up or tear yourself down with your mind. Use a positive attitude to take control of the direction of your physique and build up the confidence that will really get the show rolling. Once you get something going it will really start growing and working for you.

Vision

Part of the push of motivation, confidence, and a positive attitude comes from vision. Vision is what you want all of your goals to add up to. Vision is your ability to see the type of body that you want to shape and then to use the other disciplines to shape it in that manner. You need to envision how you will look when you get to where you want to go. The clearer your vision, the better the goals you will set to achieve that vision and the more motivated you will be to do it. Set out a clear vision of what you want to do with your body. This is not some mystical experience but rather just using your mind to paint the picture of what you want your physique to become. Buy a notebook and write down your current measurements (neck, chest, waist, arm and leg size, weight, bodyfat, etc.). Then write out what you would like to have physically – such as larger arms, a smaller waist, etc. This is the vision you want to reach for. After this you set goals to reach that vision. Those who train without a vision fail to maximize their full potential.

Sergio Oliva

Persistence

All of these traits of the mind and character are fantastic but there is one that overshadows all of them – persistence. Persistence in any area opens the door for mastery of that endeavor. This is as true in bodybuilding as it is anywhere. Persistence in training and diet is the key for changing your body from mediocre to muscular.

Vince Lombardi, the "coach" of coaches in the National Football League, would often quote this statement: "Press on: Nothing in the world can take the place of persistence. Talent will not; nothing is more common than unsuccessful individuals with talent. Genius will not; unrewarded genius is almost a proverb. Education will not; the world is full of educated derelicts. Persistence and determination alone are omnipotent."[12]

PERSISTENCE IN ANY AREA OPENS THE DOOR FOR MASTERY OF THAT ENDEAVOR.

Lee Labrada

Persistence is perhaps the best trait you can bring to bodybuilding. Often the "natural" athlete is overconfident and fails to work out as hard as needed. The underdeveloped person who applies persistence in training often overtakes and surpasses the gifted athlete. Many of the top bodybuilders, the people who have developed the best bodies, have come from a less than awesome start. Some have even had to overcome handicaps to just break even. But they persisted in their training, and built an awesome body. Training the body is more like a marathon than a sprint. There are a lot of people who get off to a hot start, but quit. Those who have a long-term attitude are the people who will build the best bodies. Put a lot of effort into being persistent and consistent in the gym and with your diet. You may have some physical disadvantages when compared to others but you can be persistent in your training and diet and persistence is the great equalizer which will allow you to catch and pass those who are not persistent. What is the strongest mental, inner trait that you can bring to the sport of bodybuilding? Probably persistence.

Knowledge
Knowledge is an essential element in any area of life, especially in bodybuilding. The more knowledgeable you are about the sport, the better progress you can make. Bodybuilding knowledge will provide you with a broad base of understanding to draw from when you are putting together your approach. Sculpting and shaping the physique is a deep subject and there is a lot to know about the human body and how it responds. Additionally, the sport of bodybuilding is a fairly new field and much information is still being discovered. A ton of research is continually being conducted in the area of fitness and the physique and it is wise to stay abreast of the latest developments. Take a tip from the champions and continually update yourself on what is going on in the world of the physique. **Dorian Yates, Lee Labrada,** and **Mike Mentzer** all dig deep in research to stay up with what is going on. You should too. This book, *Muscle Building 101,* will provide you with a solid foundation of the most essential part of bodybuilding, the basics, but there are many other good sources of information also. Bodybuilding magazines provide a consistent flow of information for all phases of physique training. Additionally, many of the champion bodybuilders have put together videos and training courses that are quite helpful for understanding many of the

Darrem Charles

YOUR MIND IS A VERY POWERFUL TOOL. USE IT TO YOUR ADVANTAGE IN BUILDING AN AWESOME BODY.

pertinent points of building the body. Study the sport of bodybuilding to know the "whats, hows, and whys" and to learn the principles and theories that have already been discovered. Much is still being discovered about building the physique but much has already been discovered and is available for your use if you dig it out of the books, magazines, training courses, and videos.

It is also a good idea to build up a body of knowledge about your physique. Your body will respond to some types of training better than it will to other types of training. You can begin to understand this by "listening to your body" (watching and noting how it does or does not respond to various changes in your workout or diet) and by trying new things now and then. It is also important to know that there is some "hype" out on the market. Every section of life has marketers and "spin doctors" who are willing to take a small portion of fact and spin a fantasy out of it. Advertising for certain bodybuilding products may or may not be true. Some advertisers stretch the truth so far that it breaks. The more you know about the fundamental truths of bodybuilding, the easier it will be to spot the phony presentations.

Your mind is a very powerful tool. Use it to your advantage in building an awesome body. The ancient Greeks and Romans were right – a strong body and mind do complement each other.

References

1. Mike Mentzer, "Heavy Duty: Mind Training," *Muscular Development* (February 1996), 188.
2. Berry DeMey, "Rx for the Mind," *Flex* (August 1990), 146.
3. Chuck Swindoll, *Victory* (Waco: Word Books, 1984), 42.
4. Garry Bartlett, "The Next Arnold?," *MuscleMag International* (April 1993), 38.
5. Overheard, *MuscleMag International* (April 1993), 251.
6. Overheard, *MuscleMag International* (April 1995), 267.
7. Norman Zale, "Sergio," *MuscleMag International* (January 1994), 35.
8. Wisdom of Grimek, *MuscleMag International* 253.
9. T.C. Luoma, "Periodization Training," *MuscleMag International* (October 1993), 94.
10. Bobby Douglas, *Take It To the Mat* (Ames, Iowa: Sigler Printing & Publishing, 1993), 137.
11. Peter McGough, "Out of the Shadow," *Flex* (August 1992), 81.
12. Swindoll, *Victory,* 43.

Dorian Yates

WEIGHTLESS WORKOUTS

One of the key pillars of building the body is weight training. However, before getting started in weight training it is wise to spend a few months (1 to 6 months) working out without weights. This type of training is not totally "weightless" since you will be using your bodyweight, but it does not involve lifting iron weights or using weightlifting machines. Another term for this type of exercise is "freehand" exercise – you perform your workouts with your bodyweight and "free hands" – no weights in them.

The freehand exercises do provide the body with some initial benefits. They challenge the muscles to a modest level of development, and prepare the body for the heavier weight training that will follow. They are also beneficial because they get the body used to pressure and balance, two areas that will become more important in weight training.

Milos Sarcev and Chris Cormier

Milos Sarcev

CHECK-UP

It is a good idea to get a green light from your doctor before beginning a workout program. Most doctors will heartily endorse your idea of working out, but need to check and make sure you don't have any limiting conditions. This is especially important if you are over 35 years of age and have not exercised for some time.

WHERE?

The freehand exercises do not involve a lot of equipment. Most of the freehand exercises can be performed at a local school playground or a park. If you have access to a chinup and dip bar at your house you can perform your workout there. You may have a friend or neighbor who has a chin-up set-up that you can use.

WHAT?

What are the specific freehand exercises? There are several basic freehand exercises that are familiar to many people. These exercises are often used in the military, for sports teams, and in martial arts.

Jumping Jacks – The jumping jack is a warmup exercise to get your body ready for further work. Stand with your hands by your sides, then jump up and bring your hands together over your head while spreading your legs out slightly beyond shoulder width, landing on outstretched feet. This is the first half of the exercise. The second is to return to the starting position. Perform several of these before you start the rest of your routine. After a few workouts you should be able to perform these for a few minutes nonstop. Perform the jumping jack on a surface that has some give to it (grass, etc.).

Pushups – The pushup is a very popular exercise and continues to find use even in the modern era of machines. The pushup primarily works the chest, shoulders, and triceps muscles of the upper body. The pushup is performed from a prone position. Push the body up to a full extension, then lower your body until the chest almost touches the ground, and repeat.

Start

Midpoint

Finish

Chinups – Another old but great exercise is the chinup. The chinup is performed in two styles – wide-grip chinups for the back muscles, and a narrow, forward-grip chinup for the biceps (arm) muscles. The wide-grip chinup is performed with a fairly wide grip (beyond shoulder width) with the palms of the hands facing outward. You can pull your body up to the front or the back (where the back of your neck almost touches the bar). This wide movement really works the back muscles. The narrow-grip chinup is performed by grasping the chinup bar with the hands 6 to 12 inches apart, palms facing you. You pull your chin over the bar, using the power of the arm's biceps muscles. Get a full extension in the down position and a full contraction in the up position for both types of chinups. It is also important to perform the chinups in a fairly smooth manner as "heaving" the body toward the bar does not build the body. Former world heavyweight boxing champion **Evander Holyfield** used the chinup in his training to help beef up his spectacular back. Natural Champion **Yohnnie Shambourger** also uses the chinup in his training and cautions others that they should avoid letting the arms do the work and focus on letting the back do all of the action.[1]

Bruce Patterson works his back muscles with wide-grip chinups.

Dips – The dip movement is a classic for building the body. To perform the dip you position your body between a dip bar or two solid surfaces of equal height that are tall enough to let you dip all the way down without touching bottom (you can bend your legs back to accommodate the height range). Dip all the way down, and then push yourself all the way back up to a full extension. Just as with the chinup, there are two types of dips. The wide dip is performed with your hands about 30 to 32 inches apart, with the head and chest tucked down and in. This exercise works the chest, especially the outer region. The other type of dip is the narrow dip, performed with the hands placed about shoulder-width apart or narrower. For the narrow dip, keep the head up and the chest out and up. This style of dip works on the triceps and shoulders. Make certain that your movements on the dip are smooth and fairly slow as you drop into the low position. Bodybuilding star **Milos Sarcev** uses weighted dips for building his triceps. Former Mr. Olympia **Larry Scott** used the wide-grip dip for working his chest at the direction of the late **Vince Gironda**.

Narrow Pushups – The narrow pushup is performed with the hands about 3 to 6 inches apart (as opposed to the regular pushup position where the hands are shoulder width or wider). This exercise works the triceps and shoulders. It may take a couple of tries to get used to the shift in balance from the regular pushup, but it is necessary to keep the hands close together to get the desired effect from this exercise.

Partial Situps – The previous exercises have primarily worked the muscles of the upper body. The next couple will focus on the waist. The situp is a famous exercise but recently has been discounted somewhat since the motion does not work the waist muscles as directly and

IT IS A GOOD IDEA TO GET THE GREEN LIGHT FROM YOUR DOCTOR BEFORE BEGINNING A WORKOUT PROGRAM.

Dips are an excellent freehand exercise for working your chest, triceps and shoulders.
– Paul DeMayo

Finish

Start

efficiently as do some variations. The partial situp is a much better exercise for tightening the midsection than is the old-style situp. The partial situp works as it sounds – you sit up part of the way. Additionally, you *do not* brace your feet. When there is no foot brace the stomach has to really work, and by not going all of the way up you remove any chance for resting.

Crunches – The crunch is the new king of midsection work. It has usurped the situp because it works the waistline much more directly than the situp does. The crunch is performed by lying horizontally, with the hands behind the head. Raise the knees (legs bent) and the head simultaneously, bringing the elbows up to touch the thighs. Hold for a two-count, then return to the starting position. British bodybuilding champion **Ian Harrison** starts his waist workout with the crunch. He likes to use a high-repetition range (20 to 30) to get an intense burn in the waist.[2]

Shawn Ray

TAKE FIVE MINUTES EVERY OTHER DAY TO PERFORM SOME STRETCHING MOVEMENTS, WORKING BOTH THE UPPER AND LOWER BODY IN A RELAXED MANNER.

Ian Harrison

One-leg Squats – The legs are trained with the one-leg squat. To squat down on both legs is quite easy but when you put the full bodyweight on one leg it provides more of a workout. Place one hand on a stationary object for balance, then squat down until your thigh is parallel with the ground. Stand up and repeat. You can hold the leg you are not using out to the front or the side. Perform this exercise for both legs.

One-leg Calf Raises – The one-leg calf raise is performed by standing on an object with a drop (such as a stair step) and lowering the body as you lower your heel. Push the body back up by moving the calf muscle all the way up. Hold in both the down and up positions for at least a two-count. Make this motion smooth and slow.

These freehand exercises should be performed together in a workout sequence. Perform the workout two or three times a week, with at least one day of rest between the workouts. A Monday-Wednesday-Friday rotation works well.

FREEHAND WORKOUT

EXERCISE	SETS	REPETITIONS
Jumping Jacks	1	2-3 minutes
Wide-grip Chinups	2	as many as possible
Narrow-grip Chinups	2	as many as possible
Wide Pushups	2	as many as possible
Narrow Pushups	2	as many as possible
Wide Dips	2	as many as possible
Narrow Dips	2	as many as possible
One-leg Squats	3-4	as many as possible
One-leg Calf Raises	3-4	as many as possible

Perform the waist work (partial situps, crunches) every morning for two sets of each for as many repetitions as possible.

You may get exhausted or have to rest during the first couple of workouts, but you will soon be able to handle this workout. Note that the repetition range is set at "as many as possible," which means this workout can be individually tailored to your level. It also requires that you be honest with yourself and push your body to the limit. Get a notebook and keep track of how many repetitions per exercise you are able to perform. Then, with each succeeding workout, you need to strive to add at least one more repetition to your maximum. This will slowly condition and build your body.

During this initial phase also engage in some aerobic/cardiovascular work. Pick an aerobic/cardio exercise that you favor (running, swimming, stationary bike, etc.) and perform it 2 or 3 times a week for at least 20 minutes nonstop. You may have to work up to the 20-minute level at first (a 10-minute workout, followed by a 15-minute workout for the next session, etc.) but aim to get up to the 20-minute minimum level.

Take five minutes every other day to perform some stretching movements, working on both the upper and lower body in a relaxed manner.

After you have worked on the freehand workout for a month or two, you can step up your level of training by making the freehand exercises more difficult. For the pushups, you can move from a flat position to a decline position. The 1995 NPC champion, **Phil Hernon,** utilizes the decline pushup. This type of pushup will put more pressure on your body and build the muscles more readily. Also try to recover more quickly between sets and don't rest as much as you did in the beginning.

Phil Hernon

FREEHAND WORKOUT 2

EXERCISE	SETS	REPETITIONS
Jumping Jacks	1	2-3 minutes
Wide-grip Chinups	3	as many as possible
Narrow-grip Chinups	2	as many as possible
Wide Pushups, declined	2	as many as possible
Narrow Pushups, declined	2	as many as possible
Wide Dips	3	as many as possible
Narrow Dips	3	as many as possible
One-leg Squats	4	as many as possible
One-leg Calf Raises	4	as many as possible

The Fundamentals of Shaping Your Physique

The exercises that have not been made more difficult by an incline position have been given an extra set. Additionally, increase the amount of sets for waist work to 3 per each exercise. Also increase the amount of time on the aerobic/cardiovascular exercise to 30 minutes per session.

Use this workout for the next 2 or 3 months. Push yourself to get in as good a condition as possible. You should be quite a bit ahead of where you were when you first started – your repetition range should be significantly higher.

The freehand exercises are fantastic for getting in general good condition. However, they can only take you so far. The principle of incremental increases ceases to be effective when you use the same bodyweight for too long. Your body weight needs to be taken to a higher level of challenge and weight training will provide the more difficult and stimulating exercise that will build a better body. Once you get free-hand exercises under your belt you will be ready to move on to the more advanced training level – iron.

You will see that a couple of the exercises in the free-hand workout will be included in the weight-training routine, but they are often done with weight added to the body (dips, etc.) and are really a weight-training movement. You can use the freehand exercises now and then as a break from weightlifting, and they work great when you are in a place that has no weights. But from now on your primary focus should be on weightlifting.

References

1. Natural Bodybuilding Stars, *Muscular Development* (December 1995), 99.
2. Ian Harrison, "The Ultimate Middleman," *Flex* (November 1995), 269.

Dorian Yates displays ultimate mass and definition in his glutes, hamstrings and calves. There is no questioning why he is a multi-Mr. Olympian.

THE MALLET OF IRON

In bodybuilding, the mallet that swings the blows and shapes the body is made of iron. Iron is the main element that is used to force the body to change shape. Perhaps it would be nice if there were an easier route, but then everyone would have a fantastic physique and it would be no big deal. But "hot" bodies are not easily attained. They come about through a lot of hard effort. To make that effort pay off, a tough tool is necessary. The tool, the hammer that strikes the blows to build the human physique, is made of iron.

Iron is compact and heavy. And for bodybuilding purposes, it is balanced. You could certainly work on the body by utilizing other material (lifting tree trunks or buckets of sand), but it would take ten times as long and not be nearly as effective. Iron is the ideal manner in which to manipulate the physique, changing it to what you want it to be.

If you have been exercising in general or with the freehand exercises you will be ready for weight training. However, the training may still come as a surprise. So don't be shocked if there is quite a bit of muscle pain. It will pass, and you will eventually become so used to it that you won't feel you have gotten a good workout unless you "feel the pain" when you train.

THE EXERCISES

There are several basic weightlifting exercises that the sport of bodybuilding employs. These exercises are the cornerstone upon which the fundamentals of the use of iron in bodybuilding are built. **Arnold Schwarzenegger** points out that there are no alternatives to the basic bodybuilding exercises.[1] Big **Michael Francois** points to the basic exercises and says, "Always remember, without a foundation you can't build a solid house."[2]

Squats – The squat has been called by many the "king of all exercises." Some trainers contend that if you could only perform one exercise, the one to choose would be the squat. **Arnold** has mentioned that a bodybuilder will always have to squat. The reason why the squat is considered so highly is that it not only works the muscles directly involved in the exercise, but it also acts as a supercharger to the rest of the body. **Achim Albrecht** agrees that squats are crucial. "When you max out with squats, not only

Michael Francois

The Fundamentals of Shaping Your Physique

do your legs grow to a far greater extent than from any other exercise, but the rest of your body appears to grow with them."[3] The squat can pack more muscle mass onto the body than any other exercise as it primarily works the largest muscle group in the body, the thighs. The squat is performed by stepping under a barbell (in a rack or on stands) with the bar riding across the back for support. Squat down until the thighs are about parallel with the floor, then push strongly back up to a standing position. It is extremely important to keep your shoulders parallel with the floor, and your chin at a level parallel or above to avoid injury. Do not squat in an unbalanced position. Good form is essential for proper squatting movements. The legs, the focus of the work of the squat, are very powerful and can handle very heavy weight in the squat, and high repetitions. When you get down to bodybuilding basics, the squat is one of the most basic. The only people who should not squat are those with a large hip/buttock area.

Almost all top bodybuilding stars have built their legs primarily with the squat. **Michael Francois** uses powerlifting squats for his mighty legs.[4] **Kevin Levrone,** runner-up in the 1995 Mr. Olympia, states that "It's important for me to designate squats as my primary leg exercise."[5]

Kevin Levrone and Paul Dillett

Bench Presses – Another exercise many claim to be the "king of all exercises" is the bench press. The bench press is the primary mass developer for the upper body. **Lee Haney, Arnold Schwarzenegger,**

and **Franco Columbu** all believed in hitting the upper body hard with the bench press. They should know – between them they hold 17 Mr. Olympia titles. The bench press works on the chest, shoulders, triceps, and back. The bench press is performed by laying flat on a bench, with a barbell supported above the bench on a pair of steel arms or in a rack. You take the barbell off and lower it until it touches your chest at around the nipple level, and then powerfully push the barbell back up to full extension. Keep your back flat and do not arch it during the bench-press exercise.

Deadlifts – The deadlift is primarily a powerlifting movement (as are bench presses and squats) but it is necessary here because it builds such a powerful foundation in the body. There are those who claim that the deadlift is the "king of all exercises." **Bill Starr,** strength and conditioning coach at Johns Hopkins University, says that "in the long list of exercises available to bodybuilders, there are only two that will effectively build greater size and strength: the full squat and the deadlift."[6] The deadlift also acts like a supercharger for stimulating muscular growth. The deadlift works primarily on the back, trapezius, thighs, and hamstrings. The deadlift is performed by bending over (with the back straight, bend at the knees) grasping the barbell at about shoulder width, and standing up. This sounds like no big deal, except for the fact that with the deadlift you really load the bar up with some heavy weight.

Shoulder Presses – The pressing motion primarily builds the shoulders and triceps. There are a variety of different pressing moves (military presses, seated presses, dumbell presses, etc., and a deadlift/press hybrid, the clean and jerk). The press is an excellent move for strengthening the shoulder region. The press is performed by lifting a barbell to shoulder level (this can be in front of the head or behind the head) and pressing the weight overhead until the arms are fully extended. Lower in a smooth motion and repeat.

Start

Finish

Paul DeMayo attacks his chest with the number one upper-body mass builder – bench presses.

> **AS LONG AS YOU ARE LOSING BODYFAT AND REPLACING IT WITH MUSCLE YOU ARE HEADED IN THE RIGHT DIRECTION.**

Curls – The curl is the basic movement for building the size of the biceps, the muscle that lies on the upper arm and which everyone flexes to show how big their arms are. The biceps is an impressive muscle, especially when fully developed. The curl exercise that develops the biceps is performed by picking up a barbell and holding it at thigh level with the palms of the hands facing out, then raising the barbell in an arc toward the chin. Keep the upper body as stationary as possible *(don't assist the motion with a little "heave")* to force the biceps muscle to do all of the work. Lower the weight back in a smooth and semi-slow action, then repeat.

Paul Dillett, the man with the 24-inch arms, points out that "for mass nothing beats the old standbys: basic heavy barbell curls and dumbell curls."[7] **Aaron Baker** uses regular barbell curls to build his fantastic arms. **Robby Robinson** built 20 1/2-inch arms at a bodyweight of only 207 pounds and one of the mainstays of his arm-training routine was the regular barbell curl.[8]

Triceps Prone Presses – The triceps prone press is a fundamental movement for developing the rear side of the arms, the triceps. The triceps prone press is performed by laying flat on a bench, face up, with a barbell in your hands above your head. Use a close grip (hands 6 to 8 inches apart) and slowly lower the barbell until it almost touches your forehead. Keep your elbows tight and close together instead of letting them flare out. The tighter the elbows, the better the effect on the triceps. Start this exercise with a fairly light barbell until you get used to the motion (you don't want to bonk your head) and can add more weight. **Sergio Oliva,** the man with arms as big as his head, used triceps prone presses to build his powerful arms.

The stiff-leg deadlift is essential if you want impressive hamstring development.
– Danny Hester

Start

Finish

The massive
Paul Dillett

Bent Rows – Bent rowing is a great way to add muscle size to the upper back area. Perform the bent rowing motion by bending forward at the waist and picking up a barbell with your hands slightly wider than shoulder width. Raise up until your upper body is just slightly past parallel with the floor, then pull the barbell into your sternum area (the place where the chest and stomach come together) and then lower to the floor. Try not to let your arms get too much involved in the pulling motion – use them as a grasping tool and let the upper back get in most of the action. **Arnold Schwarzenegger** believes that without the bent row, you cannot build a wide, muscle-studded back.[9]

Calf Raises – The calf raise is the primary manner in which to train the calf muscle, the prominent feature of the lower leg. There are a variety of manners in which to perform the calf raise, including seated and standing. The standing calf raise is performed by stepping onto a calf-raise rack and lifting the pads that are attached to a stack of weights. You lower the heel area of your foot off of the supporting platform and raise and lower the weight from the ball of your foot. Go slow, and contract and flex the muscle at the top of the movement. Go all the way down at the bottom of the rep. Go hard on the calves; they can endure a heavy workload. **Nasser El Sonbaty,** a champion bodybuilder with calves that measure more than 21 inches around, points out, "Don't be afraid to train them (calves) mercilessly – they can handle much more work than other muscle groups."[10]

Stiff-leg Deadlifts – The stiff-leg deadlift is somewhat similar to the regular deadlift with just a couple of variations. You don't bend your legs as you do in the regular deadlift (hence the name) and on the downward path of the bar you arch your head and back upward, not letting the

GET PLENTY OF REST AND RECUPERATION BETWEEN WORKOUTS. GIVE YOUR BODY A CHANCE TO REGROUP AND REPAIR ITSELF BEFORE THE NEXT BODY-CHALLENGING ROUTINE.

Start

Finish

When performing the standing calf raise, go slow, but don't forget to go hard – the calves can endure a heavy workload!
– Danny Hester

barbell travel to the floor but stopping it at about shin level. **Lee Labrada** has pointed out that going further than the shins causes another muscle group to take over, and the design for this exercise is just to go to shin level. This places the emphasis of the exercise on the hamstrings. This exercise is great for building strong and shapely hamstrings as well as working the lower back and glutes.

These exercises are the fundamental movements for building the body in the sport of bodybuilding. There are dozens and dozens of other exercises, but the fundamental concept behind each is very often based on one of the basic exercises. The exercises listed can be performed with a barbell set and bench (with the solitary exception of calf raises). You do not need a lot of fancy chrome-plated equipment to bodybuild. These basic exercises will really give your body the challenge it needs. Later on in *Muscle Building 101* more exercises will be added. For now, concentrate on building the body with these basic movements. **Lenda Murray**, multi-Ms. Olympia winner, points out that she returned to the basics for a much needed training boost which helped her grab the top title for the sixth consecutive time.[11] The basics really work.

BASIC WORKOUT

EXERCISE	SETS	REPETITIONS
Bench Presses	2	8 to 10
Shoulder Presses	2	8 to 10
Deadlifts	2	5 to 10
Triceps Prone Presses	2	8 to 10
Bent Rows	2	8 to 10
Curls	2	8 to 10
Squats	2	10 to 12
Stiff-leg Deadlifts	2	10
Calf Raises	2	12

Perform this workout twice a week, with a two-day rest between workouts.

Perform waist work on the days that you don't lift weights. Continue to perform aerobic/cardiovascular work, but cut back to 2 or 3 workouts of only 20 minutes each. Increase the time spent on stretching – stretch before, during, and after the workouts, and 5 to 10 minutes on the days that you don't work out. Take one day a week and do absolutely no training at all (not even waist).

Use the basic workout for six months straight. Add weight for any exercise in which you can reach the suggested amount of repetitions fairly easily. For instance, if you curl 60 pounds and after a few workouts can perform 10 repetitions, then add weight (5 to 10 pounds) and have another go at it. Keep doing this with each exercise as you reach the maximum suggested repetition range. You should be able to increase each of the exercises several times during the six-month time frame. Always keep track of your progress – use notebooks or training diaries to plot your progress.

Use healthy dietary habits as you train with the basic bodybuilding workout. Eat more quality protein and complex carbohydrates, and cut back on fat, alcohol, and sugar intake. Read through the upcoming chapter on bodybuilding nutrition in *Muscle Building 101* and apply the dietary guidelines given.

Get plenty of rest and recuperation between workouts. Give your body a chance to regroup and repair itself before the next body-challenging routine. Get plenty of sleep at night. Remember, your muscles grow the most during sleep.

MOVING ON

Once you have been using the basic bodybuilding routine for six months you will begin to notice some nice changes in your body. Your muscles will be growing stronger and your bodyfat levels should be decreasing. Don't be all that concerned about your bodyweight at this point. Some people take up bodybuilding to lose fat, and are quite shocked when they get on the scale after working out for several months to find out they haven't lost any weight, or may have even gained some weight. The crucial factor is body composition. A person will lose bodyfat and gain muscle. So someone who loses three pounds of bodyfat and gains five pounds of muscle will have an overall weight gain of two pounds. The point to focus on is muscle size and overall physique composition, not weight. As long as you are losing bodyfat and replacing it with muscle you are headed in the right direction.

SUPER SPLIT

Once you have the foundational training (the basics) of bodybuilding down, you can move on to some different techniques. But never stray too far from the basics. It is good to have at least one cycle per year working the basic exercises with some heavy iron. The basic movements, when performed with heavy metal, focus more on building muscle size. The more isolated and fancy movements focus more on shaping the muscles.

After the basic routine rotation, you can move on to a split rotation. The basic exercises used will be pretty much the same, but you will work with your first split set-up.

A split is a full workout divided up into various parts. A person who performs half his workout during one session and half during another is using a two-part split. And a full-body workout that is broken up into three parts is a three-part split – logical, right?

What good is a split routine? A split routine allows more time to concentrate on individual exercises. When you have all of the exercises of a routine crowded into one session you lose the ability to fully concentrate your energy on specific muscle groups. You also lose some of your energy if your workouts are too long. The workout that contains all of the exercises in one session has to be longer to get all of the training in. This drains your energy, and the exercises at the end of the session tend to be half-hearted at best. The solution is the split workout.

A workout can be split in any of dozens of ways. To initially learn the split concept, you should work with a simple two-part split – working half of the body during one workout and half during the other.

PUSH/PULL TRAINING

The workout will be split into two parts. The split is based on the push/pull concept. The push/pull concept is built on the idea of training with similar exercises (all of the pushing movements) on one day, and all of the other type of exercises (pulling motion) on a separate day.

Multi-Ms. Olympia Lenda Murray

SPLIT WORKOUT A

EXERCISE	SETS	REPETITIONS
Bench Presses	3	8 to 10
Wide Dips	1	over 10
Seated Presses	3	10
Dumbell Lateral Raisees	1	12
Narrow Dips, weighted	1	5 to 10
Triceps Prone Presses	3	10 to 12
Squats	4	15
Lunges	1	10

This workout includes a couple of exercises for each of the pushing muscle groups – the chest, shoulders, triceps, and quadriceps (frontal thigh muscles). It uses a couple of freehand exercises and one dumbell exercise. Since all of the work is directed on just these muscle groups you can really get a concentrated workout. The dumbell lateral is performed by holding a pair of fairly light dumbells and raising them out and away from the body until they are just slightly above shoulder level. If you get the position right your body will look like a "T" with a head on top. Slowly lower the dumbells and repeat. Strap some weight onto the body for the narrow dip. Rest a few minutes between working the upper body and the lower body. The lunge is performed by placing a light barbell across your back (in the same position as the squat) and stepping forward onto one foot, leaving the rear foot in place. You then push back to your original position. You do this one for both legs. Perform this part of the split workout 1 or 2 times per week.

Lee Haney

SPLIT WORKOUT B

EXERCISE	SETS	REPETITIONS
Bent Rows	3	8 to 10
Chinups	1	over 10
Curls	3	10
Dumbell Curls	1	12
Stiff-leg Deadlifts	2	12
Leg Curls	2	10
Calf Raises	2	15
Seated Calf Raises	2	10

These exercises are all pulling movements, with the exception of the calf raises, which are added here (instead of into the other workouts) to balance the training out. This workout also employs some dumbell work (dumbell curls). A weight machine is necessary for the leg curl; if you do not have access to one, perform 4 sets of the stiff-leg deadlift. Perform this workout 1 or 2 times per week, with waist workouts on the days you don't use the weight training.

This split can be performed on a one-two basis, for example: workout A on Monday, workout B on Tuesday, with Wednesday off, then workout A on Thursday, workout B on Friday, and Saturday and Sunday

Robby Robinson

off. Or you can perform workout A in the morning, workout B in the evening, and take two days off before repeating the cycle. The key point to remember is to let each specific muscle group rest for 48 hours before exercising it again.

The push/pull split is ideal for giving each muscle group maximum rest between workouts. In fact, if you use the first routine rotation mentioned you will be giving the muscles 72 hours of rest between workouts, which is ideal for maximum muscle growth. You may read in magazines or hear elsewhere that some bodybuilders lift every day, or don't give their body as much rest as recommended. However, such routines are becoming less popular as more bodybuilders are discovering the benefits of letting the body rest and recuperate.

One of the reasons why some bodybuilders, particularly the competitive bodybuilders, can use a routine rotation that is so short is because they are on anabolic steroids and human growth hormones. These drugs promote quick recovery and the building of lean muscle mass. However, they also often lead to other physical complications, and carry warning labels that list the many possible negative side effects. A young man in his 20s who had been on heavy doses of these drugs for quite some time became very sick and was told by his doctor that the insides of his body were like a 70-year-old man. These drugs can do some real damage. They are also illegal to take – you can go to jail just for possessing them. You do not need to use drugs to build an awesome body. Drugs have no place in personal bodybuilding. You are *building the body,* not tearing the body down.

The diet is the manner in which to help build the body, along with proper rest and recuperation. A great diet is the natural way for your body to build itself up without negative consequences. The following chapter will focus on the type of diet that will help you build muscles and avoid fat.

Aaron Baker

References:
1. Schwarzenegger, *Education of a Bodybuilder, 180.*
2. William Brink, "Large and in Charge," *MuscleMag International* (June 1994), 48.
3. "Death of the Squat?," *Flex* (January 1993), 148.
4. Greg Zulak, "Massive Leg Training," *MuscleMag International* (May 1993), 110.
5. "Death of the Squat?," *Flex* (January 1993), 149.
6. Bill Starr, "Dead Right," *Flex* (November 1995), 102.
7. Paul Dillett, "24 inches of Monster Meat," *Flex* (August 1992), 142.
8. Gene Mozee, "Mass from the Past," *Ironman* (October 1994), 142.
9. Schwarzenegger, *Education of a Bodybuilder,* 214.
10. Nasser El Sonbaty, "Wean Your Calves," *Flex* (January 1996), 76.
11. Lenda Murray, "Roots Revisited," *Flex* (January 1996), 94.

FOOD FOR FUEL

Greg Kovacs

Fuel is an extremely important element on planet earth. The most power-ful car in the world won't perform at all without fuel. A spaceship can go all the way to the moon and back – but it won't even leave the launching pad without fuel. Fuel is an absolute necessity for proper functioning. Without adequate fuel there is no motion.

This principle of fuel is also true for the human body. The body needs fuel to maintain and sustain its actions. Without proper fuel, the body quickly dies. For the bodybuilder, fuel is especially important. The extra hard physical demands of bodybuilding also mean that extra attention and care needs to be taken with body fuel. The body fuel for the human is the diet – the food intake.

Body fuel for the bodybuilder serves a few basic functions. The body needs food for energy. It also needs food for growth, repair, main-tenance, and the proper care of various body functions. If you want to maximize your physical potential it is essential you know and apply proper dietary rules.

> WITHOUT EXERCISE THE BODY WOULD NOT GROW MUSCULAR AND LEAN, BUT WITHOUT A PROPER DIET, THE BODY WOULD FAIL TO GROW.

Some physique trainers contend that diet is the number one element for properly building the body. The late **Vince Gironda,** for instance, believes that bodybuilding success is 85 percent nutrition. Others state that training is the chief element that builds the body. Actually, it is the balance of both. Without exercise, the body would not grow muscular and lean, but without a proper diet, the body would fail to grow. Both diet and exercise are important elements of bodybuilding. If you want to make good gains in training your body, pay close attention to this chapter on diet, and apply the nutritional approach given in the following pages.

WATER

The most vital element for the human body is water. Nothing else even comes close. Water is so important that without water you would die rapidly.

Water is not only the most abundant nutrient found in the body (accounting for roughly two-thirds of bodyweight), it is also by far the most important nutrient. Responsible for and involved in nearly every body process, including digestion, absorption, circulation, and excretion, water is the primary transporter of nutrients throughout the body and is necessary for all building functions in the body.[1]

As you can see, water is extremely important for the body. It is twice as important for bodybuilding. As mentioned, water is necessary for all of the building functions in the body. And since bodybuilding is primarily concerned with building the body, adequate water intake is crucial for the bodybuilder. To build the body properly you must drink a lot of water. Two-thirds of the body is composed of water but the muscles contain even more water – approximately 78 percent. The most abundant element in muscles, by far, is water. If you want to build your body, especially your muscles, you need a lot of water.

The importance of water can not be overemphasized in your quest for a more muscular physique.

How much water should you consume? A sedentary person is advised to take at least half a gallon of water a day. However, when you are working out you are expending more water through perspiration, and you also need more water for building the muscles back up. If you are working out, you need between one and two gallons of water per day. At first it will seem like a lot of water to be drinking, but that is because most people go around in a semidehydrated state. Your body will really appreciate the adequate provision of water and you will soon notice the positive effects. Make drinking a lot of water a constant habit. It is one of the tools for shaping the physique – a key part of the total equation for building a fantastic physique.

PROTEIN

Water is the most important nutrient. Following close on its heels is protein. Protein is the primary food element for the human body, and is of special importance to the bodybuilder. The root of the word "protein" points at its vital importance. In French, the word protein (*proteine*) means "primary substance to the body." The word protein comes from the Late Greek word *proteios*, which means "primary." That word came from an even earlier word, *protos*, which means "first." Of the food intake that the body needs, protein is of primary importance. The only thing that your body needs more than protein is water. Every person needs quality protein – the person who is building his/her body needs it twice as much. You can notice the importance of protein by looking at the Recommended Dietary Allowance (RDA) for adults as compared to children. The amount per pound of protein for children is twice as high as it is for adults. The same is true for a woman who is pregnant. Why? Because

Everyone needs quality protein – but the person who is building his body needs it twice as much.

Jeff Poulin

when the body is in a growth state it needs protein desperately. And guess what – when you are bodybuilding you are in a growth state also. You need more protein. How much do you need?

SUFFICIENT PROTEIN

The RDA for protein is 1 gram of protein for every 2 pounds of bodyweight. However, this recommendation is for the average person, who is sedentary. However, someone in training is not sedentary. A doctor noted the discrepancy and wrote:

The suggested daily requirement for protein intake is about 0.4 grams of protein per pound of ideal bodyweight. Unfortunately, these recommendations were based on studies of sedentary individuals. Recent data indicates that active people need much more. For example, Peter W. R. Lemon, PhD, from the University of Philadelphia, recommends that endurance athletes consume about 0.6 grams per pound per day, and strength athletes are advised to consume about 0.8 grams per pound per day.[2]

One of the most famous and successful bodybuilders, **Arnold Schwarzenegger,** pointed out that "protein is the most important element to the bodybuilder. Protein is for growth, maintenance, and repair of muscle tissue. The amount of protein needed by the average person is 1 gram for each 2 pounds of bodyweight. The bodybuilder needs more – approximately 1 gram of protein to each pound of bodyweight. Someone on a supergain program will require even more protein – at least 1.5 grams of protein for every pound of bodyweight."[3] If you are building your body up, working out with heavy weights, you need more protein than a sedentary person needs – much more. And you also need more than the regular athlete. A regular athlete is just taking enough protein to maintain his muscle structure. His or her main food focus is on complex carbohydrates. But a person who is building the body has a much different focus. He/she not only wants to maintain the muscle group structure – but want to increase it. That is a radically different concept than the concept of the typical athlete. A typical athlete has a concentration on an outside performance; for the bodybuilder, the body is the performance. And the protein intake level is different. Dr. Lemon suggests a range of 0.6 to 0.8 grams per pound of bodyweight for athletes while Arnold suggested 1 to 1.5 grams per pound of bodyweight for a bodybuilder.

> To build bigger muscles, you need to eat a lot of quality protein.

The minimum amount of protein you should consume is the upper end of what Dr. Lemon suggested for strength athletes – at least 0.8 grams of protein per pound of bodyweight per day. If you find you still need more muscle size, increase the amount of protein even higher, up to the limit Arnold suggested of 1.5 grams of protein per pound of bodyweight per day. Protein is essential for the bodybuilder. Former champion **Don Ross** wrote that "the diet I recommend for muscle density and natural mass production is based on high protein."[4] One doctor writes on the advantages of higher protein intake:

1. Your muscles will appear harder and fuller.
2. You will feel stronger.
3. You will notice decreased muscle soreness.
4. You will be more rested after the same recovery time.
5. You will probably observe a decrease in bodyfat.
6. You will have an increase in lean muscle mass.[5]

In addition to making certain you get enough protein (quantity) you also need to make sure that you are getting your protein from quality sources. Quality protein is protein that contains all of the eight essential amino acids. There are 22 amino acids; eight are essential. These eight essential amino acids are crucial for building muscle. Basically, plant protein sources do not contain all eight essential amino acids, but animal source proteins (meats such as beef, poultry, fish, eggs, milk products, etc.) do and are of a much higher quality.

> **Animal source proteins contain all eight essential amino acids.**

Protein must also be efficient to be effective. A food source that has 30 grams of protein but only 5 grams of assimilable protein is not as efficient as a food source that has only 24 grams of protein of which 19 of those grams are assimilable. The protein efficiency of most animal source foods is generally much higher than plant protein food sources. The top protein sources for efficiency are eggs and whey.

Bodybuilding is about reducing fat as well as building muscle, so focus on foods that are high in quality protein, yet low in fat.

If you want your muscles to grow faster, make certain you get plenty of top-quality protein in your diet. Since bodybuilding is about reducing fat as well as building muscle, don't take protein from food sources that are marbled in too much fat. Eat extra-lean beef, lean turkey and chicken cuts, fish, and skim or very low-fat dairy products. The key is to focus on foods that are high in quality protein and very low in fat. **Vince Gironda** advised taking liver tablets in addition to the daily meals to insure that you are getting enough protein. **Lee Labrada** gets much of his protein from egg whites and supplements.[6]

The Fundamentals of Shaping Your Physique

Your body can ingest 30 to 50 grams of protein per meal. Try to make certain that each meal you eat has 30 to 50 grams of high-quality protein.

MEAL FREQUENCY

The body digests food better if the food is consumed in smaller amounts. However, a bodybuilder needs a substantial amount of protein and complex carbohydrates. The compromise for the bodybuilder is to eat smaller meals, but more of them. A bodybuilder may eat 4 to 7 smaller meals per day instead of the 2 or 3 large meals that the average person eats. This allows the bodybuilder to have a constant flow of nutritious food that will provide a positive nitrogen level and a constant insulin level, both of which are vital for building the body. When you are working out hard and lifting heavy, you need to have a large and constant intake of protein. **Michael Francois** eats as many as 20 chicken breasts a day! **Mike O'Hearn** takes in about 10,000 calories a day! It takes a lot of fuel (especially protein) to build an awesome body.

Protein Shake

MAKE DRINKING A LOT OF WATER A CONSTANT HABIT.

The protein shake is the tried and true way to pack on lean muscle mass.

It is not always easy to make a meal whenever you need one; and eating, buying, preparing and storing all of those various food items can be time consuming. One of the best ways to meet your protein and caloric needs (in a quick fashion) is the protein shake. The protein shake is what most bodybuilders drink to attain some powerful protein calories. **Bill Starr** points out that the protein shake is the tried and true way to add muscle size via the diet. The protein shake is a supplement to the

diet, which adds protein without fat. A typical protein shake consists of a couple of cups of skim milk, a cup of dry milk, a couple of scoops of protein powder, along with some flavoring items such as a banana or other type of fruit. If you are really having a hard time packing on muscle size, increase the size of your protein shake. Add more milk and protein powder, along with some low-fat fruit yogurt and take a couple of shakes a day instead of just one.

EXTRA PROTEIN

Another good way in which to obtain extra protein is to take a few breaks during the day and eat a few liver tablets. Liver tablets are high in protein and B vitamins and contain quite a few other vitamins and minerals. You can ensure that you are in a positive nitrogen balance (which means your body has enough quality protein available) by taking these liver tablets. You can buy them at a local health food store.

ENERGY FUEL

Protein provides the body with the necessary nutrients for growth and building functions. But the body also needs fuel for energy. Carbohydrates provide the body with both quick energy and a slower, longer burning type of energy. Both are crucial for bodybuilding.

There are three types of carbohydrates. Fiber-type carbohydrates are the skins and bulky parts of many fruits, cereals, and vegetables. The skin from a potato or apple is an example. Fiber carbohydrates can be soluble (digestible) or insoluble (nondigestible). Both are necessary for good health. In fact when modern diets began to include more processed foods, health problems began to pop up. You need fiber. It is an important part of your daily diet. The more natural the state of the food when you eat it, the better.

The second type of carbohydrate is simple sugar. Simple sugar provides quick energy. Simple sugars, such as those found in honey and fruits, are very easily digested. Double sugars, such as table sugar, require some digestive action, but they are not nearly as complex as starches, such as those found in whole grain. Starches require prolonged enzymatic action in order to be broken down into

> ## PROTEIN IS FOR GROWTH, MAINTENANCE AND REPAIR OF MUSCLE TISSUE.

The late Don Ross

**Roland
Kickinger**

simple sugars (glucose) for digestion. All sugars and starches are converted by the body into a simple sugar such as glucose or fructose. Some of the glucose, or "blood sugar," is used as fuel by the tissues of the brain, nervous system, and muscles. A small portion of the glucose is converted to glycogen and stored by the liver and muscles; the excess is converted to fat and stored throughout the body as a reserve source of energy. When fat stores are reconverted to glucose and used for body fuel, weight loss results.[7]

You have to be careful not to get too much of your carbohydrate intake from simple sugars because any excess is stored as fat. Nutrition writer **Jay Robb** points out that "as far back as 1902 a study showed that a high-carbohydrate, low-protein diet resulted in fat deposition."[8] One of the primary goals of bodybuilding is to lower bodyfat levels. Most people eat far too much simple sugars, which of course, makes them fat.

During heavy workouts you use up your glycogen stores and leave them empty. Therefore, it is important to refuel the body and refill the glycogen stores rapidly with simple sugars. You have about two hours to replenish your glycogen with carbohydrates but the best time is within 15 to 30 minutes right after the workout. Beyond that, your intake of simple sugars should be minimal. It is easy to make the mistake of getting too much simple sugars and then having that excess turn into fat. You have to be careful because simple sugars are abundant in the tasty foods such as ice cream, cookies, and all the other goodies.

If you avoid most simple sugars, besides the time period right after a workout, what should you eat? Complex carbohydrates are the answer. Complex carbohydrates should make up a large percentage of your diet. A good bodybuilding diet is high in protein and complex carbohydrates and low in fats and refined sugars. One fitness writer notes that "complex carbohydrates ordinarily are the ideal energy source. They are slowly digested and absorbed and their calories are burned in a prolonged, even way, which provides a steady release of the critical anabolic hormone insulin."[9] The energy from the complex carbohydrate source is slowly released instead of burning up in a quick vapor as the simple sugars are. There is a much smaller chance that complex carbohydrates will be stored as fat. Complex carbohydrates are an ideal source for most of your food intake.

What are the best sources of complex carbohydrates? Potatoes (regular and sweet), yams, rice, cereals, pasta, beans, and other natural food sources provide the best choices for complex carbohydrate intake. A good bodybuilding meal has a mixture of complex carbohydrates and quality protein. A bean and low-fat beef stew would be a good example. So would a baked chicken breast with rice, or a pasta dish with turkey. A low-fat, low-sugar cereal like Grape Nuts, cream of wheat, oats, or shredded wheat with skim milk are other excellent quality protein/complex carbohydrate mixes.

Fat is a necessary part of every diet; in fact your body would malfunction without fat.

Henderson
Thorne

> **The best bodybuilding diet consists of a lot of complex carbohydrates, quality protein, and almost no fat or sugar.**

Fat tastes great – most of the foods that are the most delicious are high in fat. The juicy steak, the yummy doughnut, the potato chips, the creamy Italian butter/cheese sauce – all these enjoyable foods are full of fat. The unfortunate problem is that fat is higher – much higher – in calories than is either protein or carbohydrates. Each fat gram has 9 calories, while protein and carbohydrates contain 4 calories per gram. And fat presents another problem – it goes on to the body directly as fat. Protein and carbohydrates are first used for other functions. If there is an excess, then the excess is stored as fat. But when you eat fat, it is directly stored as fat, and the body does so easily. The use and storage of protein and carbohydrates, especially complex carbohydrates, fibers, and proteins, goes through some processes that really get the metabolism going. Not so with fat, which is easily added to the body without a lot of body action. That makes fat very dangerous – it can accumulate quickly and easily. Before you know it you have far too much bodyfat. This problem has been increasing for some time. In the 1860s fat contributed to 25 percent of the calories of the average person's diet. Today it contributes to almost 40 percent of the calories![10] Fat is fine in very small amounts, but 40 percent is far too much. So is 25 percent. A good range for the bodybuilding diet is 10 to 15 percent of calories from fat. That is not a lot of fat when compared to the average person who gets almost half of their calories from fat. It is easy to see why your body will soon look sharp.

Decreasing your fat intake will not only be better for your health, it will also make your muscles more readily apparent and shapely. Fat covers the muscles and obscures both the shape and sharpness of each muscle group.

> **Keep your fat intake between 10 and 15 percent (or lower) of total caloric intake.**

Fat on the physique, beyond the small amount necessary for certain body functions, is gross. You can burn off fat with aerobic/cardio-vascular workouts, but it is even quicker to not put on excess fat in the first place. If you keep your fat intake low, then your bodyfat level will also be low. It is that simple. Getting trim is not a hard concept to grasp – it is a hard concept to apply. One personal physique trainer noted that dieting is the toughest thing most people will do.

There are a number of quality protein sources to choose from – try a variety in your diet.

> **Getting rid of most fats and sugars in the diet is tough, but the rewards are worth it.**

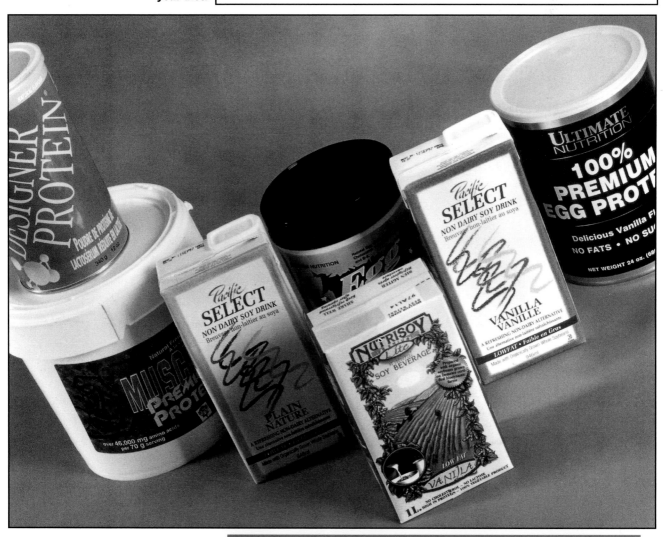

VITAMINS, MINERALS AND SUPPLEMENTS

In addition to taking plenty of complex carbohydrates and high-quality protein while avoiding sugars and fats, you also need to take in an adequate supply of vitamins and minerals. Just as a bodybuilder's needs for protein are higher than they are for the average sedentary person, vitamin and mineral needs also increase. You get quite a few vitamins and minerals in your food but to make certain that you don't miss a couple of the crucial vitamins or minerals it is a good idea to take a one-a-day vitamin and mineral supplement. You don't have to go overboard and take megadoses of various vitamins or minerals – a good one-a-day will take care of any deficiencies. Get a supplement that contains all of the necessary vitamins and minerals. And make certain that your supplement contains 100 percent of the RDA for each vitamin and mineral – some supplements don't provide a full amount. The vitamins and minerals work together in a balanced state so a one-a-day is the best way to ensure that you are not taking anything out of sync.

IF YOU ARE REALLY HAVING A HARD TIME PACKING ON MUSCLE SIZE, INCREASE THE SIZE OF YOUR PROTEIN SHAKE.

Dave Fisher

The Fundamentals of Shaping Your Physique

In addition to a one-a-day vitamin and mineral supplement, you can also provide your body with a positive nutrition boost by taking a couple of other natural supplements. These include alfalfa tablets, liver tablets, brewer's yeast (tablets or powder), and china chlorella. A steady supplementation of these super foods (which contain rich sources of vitamins, minerals, and amino acids) will benefit your body. Champion bodybuilder **Dave Fisher** notes, "I feel that supplements play a very important role in achieving the condition necessary to win bodybuilding contests." [11] Whether you are focused on winning a contest, or building your body to its ultimate potential, give your body all of the natural assistance and opportunity possible with good supplements.

FOOD LABELS

Give your body all of the natural assistance and muscle-building opportunity possible with good supplements.

To master nutrition it is essential to read food labels. Food labels tell you how much of each type of substance is in each product. The ingredients are listed in order of volume, with the item greatest listed first, and the least item listed last. The label lists vitamins and minerals, and also proteins, carbohydrates, and fats (all listed by grams).

It is important to note the type of carbohydrates listed. Most labels will break the carbohydrates into fibers, simple carbohydrates (listed as sugars) and complex carbohydrates (listed as "other" carbohydrates).

For example, a food item might contain the following label:

Fat . . . . **4 grams**
Carbohydrates . . . . **40 grams**
    sugars . . . . 3 grams
    fiber . . . . 1 gram
    other carbohydrates . . . . 36 grams
Protein . . . . **24 grams**

The total carbohydrates (40 grams in this instance) would equal the amount of all of the carbohydrates added together (sugars, fibers, and other). To find the exact percentage amount of each nutrient for this food you can measure the different types of carbohydrates against the overall percentage, and you can do the same with the individual nutrients. You can find the exact caloric percentages by multiplying each nutrient by its calories per gram.

Fat = 9 calories per gram
Carbohydrates = 4 calories per gram
Protein = 4 calories per gram

In the example listed earlier, the 36 grams of carbohydrates is divided by the 40 gram total of carbohydrates (there is no need to check percentage by caloric measure since all carbohydrates are the same per gram). This food derives 90 percent of its carbohydrates from complex carbohydrates and is an excellent source of long-term fuel.

To find the overall nutritional profile, multiply fats (this food has 4 grams of fat) by 9 for a 36 calorie total. Multiply carbohydrates (40 grams) by 4 for a 160 calorie total. Multiply protein (24 grams) by 4 for a 96 calorie total. Total all of the calories. This food has 292 calories (36 + 160 + 96). This food derives approximately: 12 percent of its calories from fat (36 divided by 292), 55 percent of its calories from carbohydrates, (160 divided by 292) which are mostly complex, and 33 percent of its calories from protein (96 divided by 292). This food would qualify as an excellent food source for a bodybuilder's diet.

Hamdullah
Aykutlu

You can determine the nutritional profile of any food by checking the label and finding out what is in it, then applying the multipliers listed above to the appropriate nutrient. The label will also provide information on the various vitamins, minerals, and other substances in the food. Learn to read and interpret labels – it will really assist you in mastering the shape and size of your physique.

Nutrition – the food you eat or don't eat plays a very large role in the control of the condition of your body. Don't neglect your diet – make it a major part of your bodybuilding program. Apply the principles listed in this chapter. Eat several small well-balanced meals (including fresh fruit and vegetables) that primarily consist of complex carbohydrates, quality protein, and little fat or sugar. Also, drink a lot of water between meals. Build your body with your diet.

Start changing your diet to make it conform with the concepts of this chapter immediately. Use it from the beginning of your bodybuilding training. Put in some time on your diet. Star bodybuilder **Mike O'Hearn** dedicates part of his day to preparing his diet.[12] So do many of the top athletes. You need to invest some time in to planning your diet. It will really pay off.

References

1. John Kirschmann, *Nutrition Almanac,* 2nd ed. (New York: McGraw-Hill, 1984), 92.
2. Christine Lydon, "Six Great Reasons to Increase Your Protein Intake," *Martial Arts Training* (November 1995), 22.
3. Arnold Schwarzenegger and Douglas Kent Hall, *Arnold: The Education of a Bodybuilder,* (New York: Wallaby Pocket Books, 1977), 152.
4. Don Ross, "Size: The Natural Approach," *Ironman* (July 1990), 103.
5. Lydon, "Protein Intake," p. 22.
6. T.C. Luoma, "The High Protein Diet," *Muscle Media 2000 (*August-September 1994),68.
7. Kirschmann, *Nutrition Almanac,* 5.
8. Jay Robb, "Fat-burning Secrets to Success," *Ironman* (October 1994), 93.
9. Chris Rand, "Nutrient Knowledge, A Guide to Building a Better Body," *Men's Workout* (September 1994), 39.
10. "Hidden Fat in the American Diet," *Nutrition 21 pamphlet,* (San Diego, 1994), 1.
11. Dave Fisher, "How I Dieted to Win My Pro Card," *MuscleMag International* (April 1995), 42.
12. Lonnie Teper, "Mike O'Hearn: Bodybuilding's Kool Kat," *Ironman* (October 1994), 148.

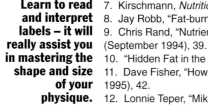

Learn to read and interpret labels – it will really assist you in mastering the shape and size of your physique.

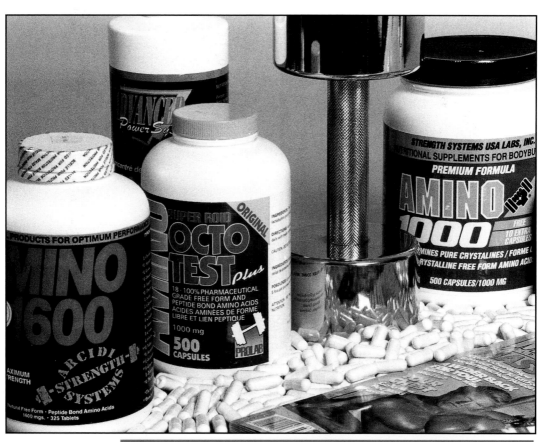

MORE METAL

Your diet is crucial if you are to have success in building your body. It is an important focus as well as lifting heavy metal. And you cannot divorce the two. Both are vital for sculpting a fantastic physique.

It is time to turn the focus back to the iron – more metal concepts. There are endless styles with which to shape the body. This chapter will focus on a few of the more major and successful training philosophies.

Once you get several months of steady training with the bodybuilding basics you will be ready to branch out and try some new training routines. Some people like to stick with the basics for one to two years, and that is great. However, variety is the spice of life, and a little change in the workout is great. This forces the body to go through what is termed "muscle confusion." The muscles get too familiar with some exercises and routines, which cause your body size and shaping efforts to plateau – to stop growing and level off. This can be frustrating because it is just at this point your interest in bodybuilding is peaking. You can beat the problem of your muscles and mind becoming accustomed and too familiar with your training by changing your workout routine. This confuses the muscles (hence the title "muscle confusion") and forces them to respond with new growth. In fact, continual progress in bodybuilding is based on finding ways to make your body continue to respond.

Arnold Schwarzenegger

Aaron Baker

THE PUMP ROUTINE

The concept of the pump has been discussed previously (the response of the muscle – engorging with blood – to certain types of training). The pump is a great way to build more muscle size and shape. Bodybuilders have been using the power of the pump for some time. Back in 1969 **Arnold Schwarzenegger** noted in a magazine, titled *Muscle Builder/Power,* "I believe that the muscles must be constantly pumped up and feel as though they have been freshly worked all day long. If there is no pump, there is no muscle growth." The pump is a crucial element to packing on muscle size. Noted physique author **Greg Zulak** points out, "Increased blood flow to a muscle is absolutely essential for growth and recovery. The proof? A muscle that pumps up easily grows easier than a muscle that does not pump up well."[1] How do you get the muscles to pump up? Super bodybuilder **Aaron Baker** writes, "I literally control biceps growth by controlling the speed of the movement and the flex of the muscle."[2]

The pump is best attained with higher repetition work. Lower repetition ranges normally do not promote a pumped muscle. The best ranges for pumping the muscle and getting the beneficial results generally come from a repetition range of 10 to 15 repetitions per set, or higher. The massive man of muscle, **Sergio Oliva,** performs 20 to 25 repetitions per set of the dip movement.[3] **Johnny Fuller** performed 32 repetitions on some exercises. However, you have to be careful. You can overdo the pump, pumping so much that the pump goes away. This can occur with extremely high-repetition ranges. For most exercises and muscle groups, a 10- to 15-repetition set works best. **Nimrod King** says, "I do 15 reps and after ten reps it's really hurting! Those extra five reps really bring out the muscularity."[4]

It is not only the repetitions that can stimulate a pump, but also the number of sets. The incredible **Serge Nubret** was famous for using light weights and a lot of sets to pump up his fantastic physique. The higher set approach is best utilized after you have some training under your belt.

The key to making the pump productive is to break through the pain barrier and get into the growth zone for a few repetitions. **Steve Davis** wrote in a triceps training article that "you must block out all mental stimuli, being conscious only of your triceps and the exercise at hand,

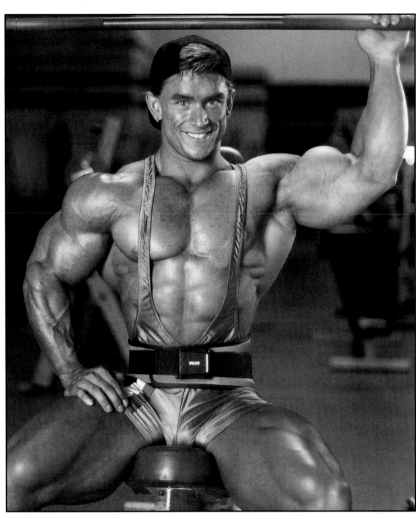

Lee Priest

focusing your creative energies on the muscle. The only muscle that moves, the only muscle that pumps, is the triceps."[5] That is a great description of how to get the pump. **Don Ross** also gives a good way to get a pump. "Slow-rep training provides not only muscular endurance, but also works the deep muscle fibers at the same time, especially with the muscle contraction at the end of every rep."[6] If you want a solid visual idea of this concept, check out the movie *Pumping Iron.* (Even the title lends itself to the pumping concept.) You can rent a copy from a local video store or buy one from a mail-order muscle magazine archive. Watch the workout sequences of the serious bodybuilders – they are really pumping the iron. Pay special attention to the squat scene with **Ed Corney** and **Arnold Schwarzenegger.** The squat is an especially painful exercise to begin with and pumping movements with the squat are really tough. Arnold forces Ed to go past the pain barrier, making him do a few extra repetitions when he is already in pain. Ed does perform the extra repetitions and you can literally see the intensity it takes to work past the pain barrier. After the workout, **Arnold** explains the concept of pumping up and getting those few extra repetitions that are so productive and make the muscles grow. Arnold notes that it is the ability to pump iron *past* the pain barrier that separates the men from the boys in the bodybuilding arena.

> **THE KEY TO MAKING THE PUMP PRODUCTIVE IS TO BREAK THROUGH THE PAIN BARRIER AND GET INTO THE GROWTH ZONE FOR A FEW REPETITIONS.**

The Fundamentals of Shaping Your Physique

For the pump to be effective, you have to use sufficient weight, which makes the muscle burn deep down during the last few repetitions. You cannot get a very productive pump without feeling some deep pain. This means you need to correlate your training poundage just right so that the last 2 to 4 repetitions are superdifficult to complete. With the idea that you need to perform 10 to 15 repetitions, you will need to correctly adjust the amount of weight you use to arrive at the pain barrier at about repetition number 8 or 9. This will take a little experimenting so don't be frustrated if you don't get it right on the first couple of attempts. You will soon become so good at finding the pain barrier that it will be no problem, no matter the exercise.

Vince Taylor

It is also important to "feel" the muscles work. **Vince Taylor** writes, "Think about 'feeling' and 'working' the muscle – not pushing a lot of weight."[7]

For pumping exercises dumbells work as well as barbells, and maybe even better since they allow for a greater isolation of the muscle groups. The form for the pump should be strict – the goal is to move the metal with muscles, not momentum. Cable movements also work well for a pump. **Vince Taylor** has used a lot of cable work in building his gargantuan arms.

One of the first things you will notice once you begin to successfully attain the pump is larger muscles! The pump expands the muscles beyond their previous capacity by quite a bit. After about an hour from the time of the pump the muscles will shrink toward the size they were before you began the day's pumping exercise, but they will remain a little bit bigger than the previous day. This small accumulation will add up once you have several pumping exercises under your belt. Some physique champions contend that the pump is totally essential for building the body's muscles beyond the basic training stages.

It is best to get the basics down before incorporating the pump approach into your routine. Once you feel the power of the pump you can get addicted, and you need to work with other styles of workouts besides just the pump. But the pump is a major part of bodybuilding and will produce some awesome results for your physique.

THE PUMP ROUTINE, Part A

EXERCISE	SETS	REPETITIONS
Incline Bench Presses	2 to 3	10 to 15
Dumbell Flyes	2 to 3	10 to 15
Dumbell Presses	2 to 3	10 to 15
Cable Lateral Raises	2 to 3	10 to 15
Cable Pulldowns	2 to 3	10 to 15
Cable Rowing	2 to 3	10 to 15
Hack Squats	2 to 3	10 to 15
Leg Extensions	2 to 3	10 to 15

Start

Finish

In addition to the pump, this routine also works on the muscle groups from different angles. It is important to stimulate the muscles from a variety of angles. Working a muscle constantly from only one groove is not a good idea. For instance, if you just use the bench press you will not really develop the upper chest region. To hit this area you need to use incline angles. The hack squat is also a different angle. This pump routine includes the flye, a dumbell movement performed by lying flat on a bench, head up, with dumbells in each hand. Extend the arms down and outward (to a level just below the bench), then bring them together up and above the head/neck area. Some have described this motion as that of hugging a very large person. The dumbell press can be performed seated or standing. The cable lateral raise is performed with one arm at a time and similar to the dumbell lateral raise. The cable pulldown is a motion that looks like a chinup but instead of bringing your body up you pull a bar attached to a weight stack down. You can pull to the front or back of the body for this movement. Cable rowing is a substitute for bent rowing, and performed seated on the floor. The leg extension is just that – extending your legs while seated on a weight machine.

Bruce Patterson gets a spot from Joanne Lee while performing an intense set of dumbell presses.

Make certain to get a good pump on each of the exercises and go past the pain barrier. Totally focus on the muscles as you move through the workout.

John Terilli demonstrates dumbell flyes in perfect form.

Start

Finish

Start

THE PUMP ROUTINE, Part B		
EXERCISE	SETS	REPETITIONS
Preacher Curls	2 to 3	10 to 15
Dumbell Incline Curls	2 to 3	10 to 15
Cable Pushdowns	2 to 3	10 to 15
Triceps Prone Presses	2 to 3	10 to 15
One-arm Dumbell Extensions	1 to 2	10 to 15
Leg Curls	3	10 to 15
Seated Calf Raises	2 to 3	10 to 15
Donkey Calf Raises	2 to 3	10 to 15

Darrem Charles pushes past the pain barrier for one final rep on the leg-extension machine.

Finish

Start

Finish

The preacher curl
is an excellent
biceps building
exercise.
– Dave Fisher

Part A of the pump workout only exercises half of the body. Part B gets the other half. The preacher curl is a curling movement performed with your arms draped over a preacher bench (slanted padded board) with a barbell. This really isolates the biceps muscles. The dumbell curl performed on an incline bench hits the biceps from a much deeper angle, stretching them a bit further than normal (which promotes more growth). The cable pushdown is like a triceps bench press, except that it is performed on a cable machine, with the hands held close together. Let the triceps do all of the work. The one-arm dumbell extension is performed with a light dumbell and you need to keep the upper arm straight up as you lower and raise the dumbell with sheer triceps power.

Start

Finish

Lee Labrada
performs incline
dumbell curls
with straight-out
intensity.

The Fundamentals of Shaping Your Physique

Standing leg curls are one variation of the leg-curl machine, allowing you to work one leg at a time.
– Matt McLaughlin

Start

Finish

The leg curl is performed on a leg-curl machine. Make certain to keep your hips tight against the padded machine as you raise and lower the attached weight. The seated calf raise is similar in motion to the calf raise except for the fact that you are seated. The donkey calf raise is performed by bending over at the waist with the ball of the foot supported on a raised platform and the heel of the foot off the edge of the platform. Support yourself by placing your elbows on a stationary object. Have someone sit across your back, and raise up and down with your calves. As with the first pump workout, make certain to take each exercise into the pain zone with the higher repetition range and a lot of intense concentration.

Perform each of these workouts twice a week, with at least a couple of days rest before you repeat the same workout. Use the pump workout for a few months and note your results. Once you get into the pump groove you won't forget it.

THE POWER WORKOUT

Although some bodybuilders swear by the pump workout, others swear by the power workout. Since both are beneficial you should spend time on each. The concept behind the power workout is that in order for a muscle to grow bigger it must grow stronger. **Craig Titus** says, "The stronger a muscle gets the bigger it gets, all things being equal. That's why I always strive to handle more and more weight and to get stronger and stronger. I know that as long as my weights keep going up, my muscles are going to get bigger."[8] **Lou Ferrigno** says that "to become as powerful as you look, you will actually have to train specifically for strength. To gain strength, you must train very heavy with low reps for one or two basic exercises."[9] **Franco Santoriello** notes, "I train heavier and slower in the off-season, with more rest between sets and not so many supersets, because I feel you need the heavy weight to grow."[10] And stronger muscles are developed through heavy-duty weights. The man with the most top titles, Mr. Olympia **Lee Haney,** is a big believer in power workouts. Some bodybuilders use a power workout earlier in the year or during off-season training, but not Lee. He uses power workouts all year long. And they paid off for him. Lee is big and muscular all year, and he won eight Mr. Olympia titles, more than any other bodybuilder. Another Mr. Olympia champion, **Franco Columbu,** is also a very strong advocate of power workouts. **Arnold Schwarzenegger** used more pumping workouts toward the end of his career, but in his formative stage he used power movements. **Reg Park** used very heavy power workouts for his movie star physique. **J.J. Marsh** believes that "sometimes a person has to go heavy in the off-season to gain additional size and strength."[11] Big **Gary Strydom** uses heavy basic exercises to build mass.[12] **Eddie Robinson** is emphatic when he says "I believe in blasting . . . the only way you're going to grow is to tighten everything, overload the muscle and do whatever it takes to get the weight up there."[13] Going heavy produces some significant results for most people.

Some people seem to grow better from pump workouts; others make better gains from the power movements. Use at least a couple of cycles of each to determine which works best for your body.

The repetition range for the power workout is 5 to 7 repetitions per set. Occasionally when you are using very heavy weights you can go with an even lower repetition range (1 to 3) but generally try to stay within the 5- to 7-rep range.

Since you are using a lower repetition range you can use heavier weights. The heavy weights force the body to respond rapidly with strength and size gains. The best exercises for power workouts are basic compound movements. Compound movements involve several muscle groups as opposed to the isolation workouts. However, an occasional heavy-duty isolation workout can also produce some gains.

Craig Titus

The Fundamentals of Shaping Your Physique

THE POWER WORKOUT, Part A

EXERCISE	SETS	REPETITIONS
Heavy Bench Presses	2 to 3	5 to 7
Heavy Flyes	2	5 to 7
Clean and Jerks	2	5 to 7
Heavy Behind-the-head Presses	2	5 to 7
Deadlifts	1 to 2	5 to 7
Heavy Curls	3	5 to 7
Stiff-leg Deadlifts	2	7 to 10
Standing Calf Raises	2 to 3	7 to 10

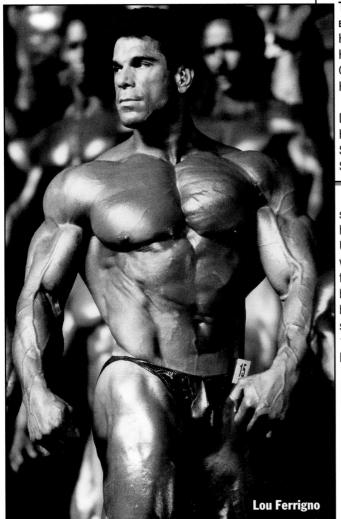

Lou Ferrigno

The leg movements in this routine have a slightly higher repetition range since the legs can handle heavier weights with a higher rep count. Use each exercise for up to seven repetitions, then when you have become used to using the weight for seven repetitions, add more weight and strive to bring your repetition count up to the target range of between five and seven. Rest a little more between sets to generate maximum power. Use this workout 1 or 2 times a week in conjunction with the second half of the power workout routine, which is part B.

THE POWER WORKOUT, Part B

EXERCISE	SETS	REPETITIONS
Heavy Triceps Bench Presses	2 to 3	5 to 7
Heavy Dips, weighted	2	5 to 7
Chinups, weighted	2	5 to 7
Heavy T-bar Rowing	2	5 to 7
Heavy Squats	3	7 to 10

This workout is not as long but the heavy squats at the end will really tax your body. Perform it 1 or 2 times a week.

When on the power routine aim at increasing the amount of weight you are using, but also keep your form fairly strict. It is easy to start getting sloppy with the heavy weights, and when you do you open your body up to the possibility of an injury. Adherence to strict form will keep you from making a mistake which could cause an injury. Train heavy but train smart.

COMBO

Some bodybuilders incorporate a pump workout with a power workout in the same routine. This power/pump combination is actually a very good way to give the body the best of both worlds. **J.J. Marsh,** who advocates power workouts, also mentions the necessity of including high volume exercise with the power workouts.[14] **Michael Francois** also believes in a mixture. He notes that "the first exercise is slow and heavy, powerlifting style, and the next two or three exercises will be lighter and faster paced."[15] A combined workout really works great when you want to fully hit the body.

TOTALLY FOCUS ON THE MUSCLES AS YOU MOVE THROUGH THE WORKOUT.

Eddie Robinson

THE POWER/PUMP COMBO WORKOUT, Part A		
EXERCISE	SETS	REPETITIONS
Heavy Bench Presses	2 to 3	5 to 7
Incline Dumbell Presses	3	10 to 15
Heavy Presses	2	5 to 7
Dumbell Lateral Raises	3	10 to 15
Heavy Curls	2 to 3	5 to 7
Preacher Curls	2 to 3	10 to 15
Stiff-leg Deadlifts	2	7 to 10
Leg Curls	2	10 to 15
Seated Calf Raises	4	15 to 20

Perform this workout 1 or 2 times a week. The power/pump workout lets you work both types of muscle fibers (fast twitch fibers = heavy training; slow twitch fibers = pump training) in one routine. This combination workout is an excellent overall training routine and you can use it throughout the year. Many of the top bodybuilders use a similar mixed approach.

This mixture of heavy power movements with lighter, higher repetition pump movements is also used for the second part of the workout. You can perform either workout first during the week; the key is to get at least a couple days of rest before using the same workout again.

THE POWER/PUMP COMBO WORKOUT, Part B		
EXERCISE	SETS	REPETITIONS
Heavy Triceps Bench Presses	2 to 3	5 to 7
Triceps Cable Pushdowns	3	10 to 15
Heavy Cable Pulldowns	2	5 to 7
Cable Rowing	3	10 to 15
Heavy Leg Presses	2 to 3	5 to 7
Leg Extensions	2 to 3	10 to 15
Lunges	1	15

Hit this workout 1 to 2 times a week also. The combination workout is perhaps the best overall workout approach since it gives the body a dual challenge – pump and power movements.

MAKE YOUR OWN ROUTINE

After you have been working out for some time you will have developed the bodybuilding acumen to put together your own workout. You will come to know what does and doesn't work for your unique physique. As you work out on a consistent basis you will develop an insight and physique understanding, allowing you to fashion your own routines. Before you attempt that, it is a good idea to know which exercises work best for the major muscle groups.

Hamdullah Aykutlu

Neck – Neck raises with a strap attachment, four-way neck machine, towel pulls.

Upper Chest – Incline-bench presses, incline dumbell presses, incline dumbell flyes, incline dumbell twists, decline pushups, high arc flyes.

Middle Chest – Bench presses, flyes, dumbell bench presses.

Inner Chest – Pec-dek machine, close-grip bench presses.

Outer Chest – Wide-grip dips, cable crossovers.

Lower Chest – Decline-bench presses, decline dumbell presses.

Shoulders – Behind-the-head presses, front presses, dumbell presses.

Front Deltoid – Barbell front raises, dumbell front raises, bench presses.

Side Deltoid – Dumbell lateral raises, reverse lateral raises, cable raises, wide upright rows.

Rear Deltoid – Dumbell bent lateral raises, bent cable raises.

Trapezius – Shoulder shrugs, deadlifts, dumbell shoulder shrugs, upright rows (narrow).

Upper Back – Chinups, cable pulldowns, pullover machine.

Middle Back – Bent rowing, cable rowing, T-bar rowing, one-arm T-bar rowing, dumbell rowing, medium-grip cable pulldowns, Hammer machine rowing.

Lower Back – Stiff-leg deadlifts, good morning exercise, hyperextensions.

Biceps – Curls, dumbell curls, incline dumbell curls, preacher curls, EZ-bar curls, narrow-grip curls, reverse curls, hammer curls, cable curls, narrow-grip chinups.

Triceps – Triceps bench presses, narrow dips, cable pushdowns, dumbell kickbacks, triceps prone presses, one-arm extensions, standing French presses, narrow pushups, prone dumbell extensions, kneeling cable extensions.

Quadriceps – Squats, front squats, hack squats, leg presses, sissy squats, leg extensions, lunges.

Hamstrings – Stiff-leg deadlifts, leg curls, single-leg curls.

Calves – Standing calf raises, seated calf raises, donkey calf raises, press-machine calf raises, one-leg dumbell calf raises.

Waist – Crunches, partial situps, leg raises, V-raises, bicycle crunches, extended crunches.

Forearm – Reverse curls, hammer curls, wrist curls, reverse wrist curls, hand gripper exercises, putty exercises, weight roll-ups, deadlifts.

Bruce Patterson

These are some of the more popular and productive exercises for the major muscle groups – there are many more exercises that will also work. You may discover an exercise that works great for your body that is not mentioned here. If it works for you, then use it. Bodybuilding is a very pragmatic sport. If something works, use it, regardless of any other concepts or theories. Some exercises may work great for one bodybuilder, yet poorly for another. If it works for you – use it!

EXPERIMENTATION

If you have been using some of the various workouts described in *Muscle Building 101* and are starting to get a good feel for the sport of weight training you can begin experimenting with your workouts. **Sergio Oliva** points out, "You won't know what's best for you until you've tried several routines, several exercises, and several exercise combinations."[16] You may perform your workouts in any way you want provided you use the know principles correctly. For instance, you can use a workout like the power workout in any weekly rotation you want, but use

Mohamed Makkawy,
Gunther Schlierkamp,
Chris Cormier and
John Simmonds

THE BETTER YOU ARE ABLE TO KNOW AND APPLY THE TRAINING CONCEPTS FROM MUSCLE BUILDING 101, THE BETTER YOUR PROGRESS WILL BE.

it in a manner that provides adequate rest between workouts. You cannot get around the physical rules of the universe. That is, if you drop a weight, it goes down, not up. When you train the body with a superhard workout, it needs a day or two to recover before you do it again. So set your workouts up in a fashion that suits you, but don't break any known principles. (The basic principles are outlined in chapter two.)

EXCEPTIONS

With every rule there is an exception or two. This is also true in body-building. You should always follow the basic principles except for an occasional *deliberate* change of pace. These times when you change the pace are great for *shocking* the body into new growth. The body can become too familiar with your workout pattern to provide new muscularity. You must trick it with a new training technique. One of the first proponents of the shocking theory was Arnold Schwarzenegger. He stated:

I finally arrived at the idea of shocking the muscles. If you do ten sets of bench presses or any other exercise regularly for a year, the muscles gradually get used to ten sets of bench presses and the growth slows down. So once a week I took a training partner and drove out into the country with the weights. We limited ourselves to one exercise for a particular bodypart. I remember for the first day we carried 250 pounds out into the forest and did squats for three hours straight. I began by doing twenty repetitions with 250 pounds; then my partner did whatever he could. Then it was my turn again. We ended up doing something like fifty-five sets of squats each. The last hour seemed endless. But it worked. Our thighs pumped up like balloons. That first day we gave our thigh muscles such a shock that we couldn't walk right for a week. We barely could crawl. Our legs had never experienced anything as tough as those fifty-five sets. And each of us put something like an eighth or a quarter inch on our thighs; they just blew up, they had no chance to survive except to grow.[17]

This approach may seem radical, but it often takes a radical approach to get the muscles growing again once you have plateaued. You can select any bodypart and blow it out with *shock* training. Of course, you do not want to make this workout style the norm since you would soon deplete your body's reserves, but it works great as a jump-start when your progress stalls. Another way to employ this *shocking* tactic is to take a bodypart and perform 1 or 2 sets for that bodypart every hour of the day for a full 8 to 10 hours. You simply go in and perform the exercise, then go back to whatever you were doing, and repeat this every hour on the hour. Of course, this works best on a day off (unless your boss lets you take weights to work!). The concept behind the *shock* approach is that it is done infrequently; the more frequent you use the shock approach the less effective it is. So try it, but don't overdo it. Most of the current research in bodybuilding is pointing to the idea that most bodybuilders need more rest and recuperation, not less.

Berry DeMey

THE HARDGAINER

Another school of thought surrounds the idea of the "hardgainer." This concept focuses on the fact that some people have a very difficult time gaining muscle size with the standard approach and need different tactics to make significant gains. The hardgainer has a physique that is not "genetically gifted." The "hardgainer" approach is to avoid the pump-style workouts, and to avoid the long, drawn-out marathon workouts which deplete the recovery system. The hardgainer uses brief, abbreviated training with fairly heavy weights, focused on basic movements. If you find that the standard workouts are not bringing results (after a year or two) you might want to give the hardgainer approach a whirl.

LOW-SETS VS. HIGH-SETS TRAINING

An area of controversy about the correct training approach, which has continued to divide the sport, is that of the low-set vs. high-set training style. Some bodybuilders advocate performing just a few sets (sometimes as low as one) per exercise and only a couple of exercises per bodypart. Arthur Jones, who developed the Nautilus training equipment,

The Fundamentals of Shaping Your Physique

was one of those who introduced this approach. It gained steam when Mike Mentzer, a multi-title champion, adapted it to his training, with some impressive results. This type of training recently received a boost when the current multi-Mr. Olympia winner, massive Dorian Yates, also adopted it as his approach. The idea behind this type of training is to use 1 or 2 sets at 100 percent maximum effort to force muscle gains.

The other approach is to use many sets per exercise per bodypart. The output is generally at 70 to 90 percent of maximum effort for several sets. Some advocates of this style of training use double-digit sets per bodypart. This approach also has notable users, such as **Arnold Schwarzenegger, Lee Haney, Franco Columbu, Sergio Oliva,** (all multi-Mr. Olympia winners) and many others. Most bodybuilders use the multiset-per-exercise-per-bodypart approach but more are starting to try the single-set theory as **Dorian Yates** continues to rack up consecutive titles with this type of training.

Joe Spinello

What should you use? Give both a try. It is never wise to bury your head in the sand. Try both styles and see which one works for you.

MASS VS. AESTHETICS

Another dividing line in the sport of bodybuilding is that of mass vs. aesthetics. The proponents of muscle mass are those who believe in size at all costs. The aesthetic camp believes that muscles should be symmetrical, proportionate, and that shape is more important than size. This area of bodybuilding is one of personal preference. You decide what you want for your body and head in that direction. You can focus on building muscle mass (with heavy-duty training, less aerobic/cardiovascular work, and heavy-duty diet) or you can focus on shaping the muscles into a leaner look (with specific shape weight training, more stretching, more aerobic/cardiovascular work, and a light yet nourishing diet). Both sides of the debate are correct – mass looks great, and so does shape. You choose which way you want to proceed with your training goals.

As you may have noticed, much of bodybuilding involves the freedom of choosing what type of physique you want to fashion. Do you want to build a body with bigger and more massive muscles, or do you want a physique that is lean and mean – trimmer and tight? The choice is yours. Perhaps you feel that your lower body is fine, but your upper body needs more muscularity. Or perhaps the reverse is true. You can work the whole body, or just specific parts. Bodybuilding is a fantastic way to work the body into just what you want it to be. Personal bodybuilding is the best approach of all.

By knowing as much as possible about the various concepts, theories, and applications of the sport of bodybuilding, you will provide yourself with a wider range of material to use. The more information and data you have at your disposal, the more informed choices you can make. This is true in any area of life; it works just as well in bodybuilding. Try the various concepts and use them to build the body you want.

PYRAMID

One of the concepts that can really help you increase your muscle size and strength is the pyramid concept. The fantastic physique of **Sergio Oliva** was developed with a pyramid approach. The pyramid concept is applied to each exercise at the set and repetition level. Some people put a weight on a barbell, dumbell, or weight machine, and use the same amount of weight for the same amount of sets all of the time. This works for producing gains initially, but the body quickly adapts, giving no more advances. To overcome this problem, you can use a pyramid-set workout. A lot of bodybuilders use the pyramid-set approach to push their physique to higher levels. It is one of the favorite manners in which

Melissa Coates

to train and can be applied to any bodypart. To perform the pyramid-set workout, you start with a lighter weight and use higher repetitions for the initial set – basically a warmup. With each succeeding set you add weight, and naturally, decrease the repetitions. The following is an example of the pyramid set applied to a curl exercise:

Pyramid Set
warmup = 55 pounds x 15 repetitions
second set = 70 pounds x 12 repetitions
third set = 80 pounds x 10 repetitions
fourth set = 90 pounds x 8 repetitions
fifth set = 80 pounds x 9 repetitions
sixth set = 70 pounds x 10 repetitions

There are many variations of the pyramid. Some use only the first half of the pyramid.

Half-pyramid Set
warmup = 55 pounds x 15 repetitions
second set = 70 pounds x 12 repetitions
third set = 80 pounds x 10 repetitions
fourth set = 90 pounds x 8 repetitions
fifth set = 100 pounds x 6 repetitions

Those who only use the first half of the pyramid sometimes stop on the heaviest set, or they sometimes will finish the exercise off by building up to the heavy set and then concluding with a lighter set (in this example, perhaps 60 pounds x 12 repetitions). There is a tremendous amount of variety possible.

The Fundamentals of Shaping Your Physique

Lee Priest

You can also use this style for approaching your maximum poundages in any particular movement.

HEAVY METAL

Although bodybuilding does not focus solely on weight training, pumping iron is the hub around which the full wheel of bodybuilding turns. To make significant changes in the physique, it is absolutely essential to use the tools that weight training provides. The better you are able to know and apply these training concepts, the better your progress will be. Use the various techniques and concepts to build your body to the fantastic level you desire. Heavy metal is the way to go!

References

1. Greg Zulak, "Pumping Blood!," *MuscleMag International* (May 1988), 33.
2. Aaron Baker, "Deliberate Contractions," *Flex* (August 1990), 63.
3. Norman Zale, "Sergio," *MuscleMag International* (January 1994), 35.
4. Greg Zulak, "Building King Size Delts," *MuscleMag International* (March 1990), 91.
5. Steve Davis, "Iso-Tension Triceps Training," *Ironman* (September 1994), 69.
6. Don Ross, "Slow Down and Grow," *MuscleMag International* (March 1990), 62.
7. Reg Bradford, "Vince Taylor's Huge, Massive, Freaky Arm Routine," *Muscular Development* (February 1996), 60.
8. Greg Zulak, "A Heavy Weight Affair," *MuscleMag International* (January 1994), 54.
9. Lou Ferrigno, "Training Rap," *Flex* (July 1985), 10.
10. Greg Zulak, "Blast Your Chest My Way," *MuscleMag International* (January 1994), 98.
11. Gayle Hall, "J.J. March… The 3:30 AM Warrior," *MuscleMag International* (December 1990), 54.
12. Don Ross, "Gary Strydom," *MuscleMag International* (July 1989), 26.
13. Eddie Robinson, "Ed and Shoulders," *Flex* (November 1995), 67.
14. Hall, " Warrior," 54.
15. Greg Zulak, "Massive Leg Training," *MuscleMag International* (May 1993), 111.
16. Rick Wayne, "My Real Training Methods," *Flex* (July 1985), 104.
17. Arnold Schwarzenegger and Douglas Kent Hall, *Arnold: The Education of a Bodybuilder,* (New York: Wallaby Pocket Books, 1977), 84.

ESSENTIAL ELEMENTS

Lifting weights and eating a specific, nutritious diet are the two main components of bodybuilding. But they are not the only elements which make up this awesome sport. There are a few other "essential elements," items that are important enough to be considered part of the foundational structure of the sport. Bodybuilding is not a one-element sport as so many are – it consists of various facets. And this chapter will focus on some of these vital elements. In order to make maximum progress, it is important to include these elements in your approach to building your body. You have to go beyond just pumping iron and eating specific nutritious food. You can learn what these "extras" are in the following pages.

REST AND RECUPERATION

The human body needs a certain amount of sleep. This varies by individual, but everyone needs some sleep. It is during the sleep phase that most growth and repair occurs. Without adequate sleep the body soon falls into massive disrepair. **Lee Labrada** states, "The body needs rest in order to adapt to the stress you are putting on it in the gym – that is, you need plenty of rest time for muscular hypertrophy to occur."[1]

Aaron Baker

Garrett Downing

For the bodybuilder, adequate sleep is very important since most growth and repair occurs during sleep. The bodybuilder desperately needs this sleep time since his or her body is in a constant state of needing repair, and growth. If you were to lift weights on a steady basis and not get any real amount of sleep, your body would fall apart. The weight-training time tears the muscle tissue down (partially) and the diet provides the necessary material for repair, but it is during sleep that the repair and new growth occur. Therefore, sleep is as vital to building the body as is weight training and diet. You cannot have any of these three alone, or even any two. It is crucial you give adequate time and priority to all three, including rest and recuperation.

Sleeping at night is the primary manner in which to let the body repair and rebuild. However, you can assist this process by taking an occasional nap, and by taking some time off each week just to take it easy and rest. The adage, "a bow that is always bent soon breaks" is true. You cannot run the body at full throttle all of the time. You do have to kick back on occasion, and relax. Let the body get into a good rhythm of work and rest. If the average person needs adequate rest, how much more does the person who is lifting tons of metal? Make rest and recuperation an important priority in your day.

How much? Since everyone is unique, the amount of rest you need will vary from person to person. A suggested range is 7 to 8 hours per night. Some people need more than this, and others get by on less. Generally, when you are in a growth state, you will need more rest, not less. It is particularly important to get extra sleep when in the initial stages of bodybuilding and during mass size routines.

AEROBIC/CARDIOVASCULAR CONDITIONING

Another essential element of bodybuilding is aerobic/cardiovascular conditioning. **Tom Platz** believes that "aerobic training in addition to bodybuilding workouts is absolutely essential during a peaking cycle in order to metabolize stored bodyfat. Indeed, the three factors that have resulted in the most massive and ripped-up physiques of today are heavy, high-intensity bodybuilding training, a low-fat diet, and plenty of aerobic exercise."[2] Eating right helps keep fat off of the body, and a good aerobic/cardio program burns off any fat that sneaks onto the body. Aerobic/cardiovascular conditioning is essential for the heart. For instance, as many as 12 percent of all deaths in the United States may be attributed to lack of regular physical activity.[3] Aerobic/cardio activity is essential; it builds the long-term health of the heart. Additionally, aerobic/

YOU HAVE TO GO BEYOND JUST PUMPING IRON AND EATING SPECIFIC NUTRITIOUS FOOD.

cardiovascular work strengthens all of the major systems of the body and gives the physique much more endurance. A bodybuilder who has been using aerobic/cardio conditioning has more endurance when training with weights and receives more benefits than does the bodybuilder who neglects aerobic/cardiovascular work. Last, but not least, is that a bodybuilder who regularly incorporates aerobic/cardiovascular work into his or her routine has a body that looks better – healthier, leaner, tighter, more graceful and naturally appealing.

However, there is a caution for bodybuilders when it comes to aerobic/cardiovascular conditioning. Although aerobic/ cardio work is essential, too much of it can be detrimental. Your body has only so much energy, fuel, and recuperative powers available, and you don't want to expend all of them on aerobic/cardiovascular work. You need most of your energy and repair stores to be spent on pumping iron, not pumping your legs. Long, continuous, hard aerobic/cardiovascular workouts can actually hinder your bodybuilding progress. The key is to perform the aerobic/cardiovascular work in shorter periods (20 to 45 minutes) and to choose aerobic/cardiovascular work that does not push the body too far. One exercise that most bodybuilders avoid is long-distance running. This depletes

Serge Nubret

the system and can cause loss of muscle mass. (How many "buff" long-distance runners do you know – and how big are the biceps of a marathon runner, if you can find them?) There are some specific aerobic/cardio exercises that many bodybuilders use to burn off bodyfat and build endurance without pushing the body too far. These favorites include stair stepping, the stationary bike, and power walking. These exercises can be performed at a steady and nonstop continuous rate, elevating the heart beat to around 60 to 70 percent of the maximum (the best range to burn off bodyfat), yet not push the body too far into overdrive, where muscle tissue is lost.

Power walking is a particularly excellent exercise for the body-builder. It is performed at a brisk pace (a pace similar to a march) and for a long period of time. The best speed for an effective power walk is around 3.5 to 4.5 miles per hour. And you need to keep this rate up for around half an hour. Your body does not begin to burn fat as fuel until you have been exercising for at least 20 minutes. For a power walk to be effective you need to perform it for a minimum of 30 minutes. A longer walk is even better.

How often should you perform aerobic/cardiovascular exercise? A minimum of 3 workouts per week is suggested by most aerobic-style trainers. However, in the initial stages of building your body and during periods when you are focusing on mass training, a couple of workouts a week should be enough. Once you have built up a good base of muscle mass, you can increase the amount and time of the aerobic/cardio work you perform – to as high as 3 to 5 workouts a week, from 30 to 60

MAKE GOOD POSTURE A HABIT AND IT WILL MAKE YOUR PHYSIQUE APPEAR EVEN MORE IMPRESSIVE.

Sue Price

> **Weight training is primarily a muscle-building activity, not a fat-burning exercise. To burn off bodyfat you need to perform aerobic/cardiovascular exercise in addition to weight training.**

minutes per workout. But remember, this is after you have built up a firm foundation of muscle mass. Until that time, aerobic/cardio work should be performed in moderation.

POSTURE

How would you like to look better instantly? You can, by utilizing your posture. As mentioned earlier, bodybuilding is not all weight training and diet. Another aspect of the physique is how you carry it.

Good posture allows for better breathing and appearance. It helps the lungs, the spine, and muscles of the neck and back. A bodybuilder **Dennis Newman**

with a great physique but who has poor posture detracts from his overall appearance. What is good posture? Holding the shoulders square, the chest and chin up, the waist in, sitting up, and not slouching. Make good posture a habit and it will make your physique appear even more impressive.

POSING

Posing is the art of presenting the physique at its best. The sport of bodybuilding includes posing at the competitive level. The pose is how a bodybuilder displays the body. There are a variety of poses that a body-builder will use to show off the body from various angles. A bodybuilding competition has several mandatory poses, which a bodybuilder must present to the judges so that they can compare one physique with another. There is also an oppor-tunity for bodybuilders to pose however they choose, and a "posedown" at the end of the contest where the top finalists compare their best poses with one another.

Does a pose have any place in personal bodybuilding if you have no plans to enter a contest? Surprisingly, it does. Posing can help you direct the

Kevin Levrone

blood flow to the muscle group you are focusing on. By flexing and contracting the muscles at an all-out effort, you stretch the muscles at both ends of the movement in a maximum manner. Posing in front of a mirror can help because you get to see the results and watch as you literally "make the muscles move." Muscle control helps the muscles grow in the way you want them to, and posing is the best manner in which to control the muscles. Pose often for maximum development.

STRETCHING

Another useful training tool for bodybuilding is stretching. Bodybuilders stretch to increase their muscle range and allow for more size to be built into the muscles. Many of the top bodybuilders have noted that their muscles took off like a rocket when they started stretching. **Lenda Murray** credits stretching for turning her physique into fantastic condition.

Stretching is best done in two periods. One combines stretching directly before, during, and after each exercise. While you rest between sets and exercises you should stretch the muscles that are being used. And the other time is on off-days, when you are not training. You don't need a major time expenditure to get in some good stretching. Spend about five minutes on the upper body and five minutes on the lower body. Stretching may not seem like a big deal, but it will add another dimension to your training and appearance.

BODY SIZE

Throughout your training make certain to occasionally check your body measurements. Weigh yourself, measure your major muscle groups, check your bodyfat percentage, and watch the mirror. These measures and checking maneuvres allow you to stay on top of what is going on with your physique. You can check your bodyfat percentage with a caliper or at a local health clinic or at a college with a health program. Keep a notebook and chart your progress. This can be very encouraging and allows you to see just how drastic a change bodybuilding can bring to the body.

Garrett Downing

STRETCHING MAY NOT SOUND LIKE A BIG DEAL, BUT IT WILL ADD ANOTHER DIMENSION TO YOUR TRAINING AND APPEARANCE,

PARTNER?

Should you train with a training partner? The choice is up to you. If you are lifting heavy metal, then the choice is a no-brainer – you need a spotter. But for most training the use of a training partner is optional. A good partner can encourage you at the right times and push you to achieve new levels. A poor partner can detract from your training. Training alone allows for greater concentration. Sometimes a training partner is late (coming to the gym) or talks too much during the workout. On the other hand, sometimes when you train alone you don't push yourself to the limit. Both choices have positive and negative aspects you need to consider.

The Fundamentals of Shaping Your Physique

Training alone or with a partner is an option that is up to you. Trial and error will point out the right path for you to take.

SYNERGISM

Bodybuilding is not a one-horse show. It includes a variety of different elements which all contribute to the full process. The major elements of bodybuilding are weight training, diet and rest. They are supported by even more elements (aerobic/cardiovascular training, stretching, etc.) which optimize your training. When all of these elements are combined together, the results they produce are greater than their individual parts. This synergistic effect speeds the whole process along at a quick pace. To make the most of your physical potential use all of the essential elements of body-building.

Edgar Fletcher

BODYBUILDING -- KING OF FITNESS

There are dozens of different fitness approaches available for you to use on your physique. Most of them do provide some benefits. However, if you want to take maximum control of your body, bodybuild-ing is the best training approach to use. It is the most advanced manner in which to totally take the initiative in making your body into what you want it to be. Use the information in *Muscle Building 101* to pass your physique course and build an awesome body!

References

1. Lee Labrada and Carol Ann Weber, "How I Packed Extra Muscle on My Back," *MuscleMag International* (August 1994), 80.
2. Overheard, *MuscleMag International* (May 1988), 93.
3. The University of California at Berkeley Wellness Letter, quoted in *Let's Live* (August 1995), 10.

INDEX

Contributing Photographers
Jim Amentler, Irvin Gelb,
Robert Kennedy, Jason Mathas,
Mitsuru Okabe, Josef Adlt,
Artie Zeller